BECOMING A MASTER OF DIVINE CONSCIOUSNESS

"Keys to bring balance to your emotion's and thoughts"

Nikki G. MCcray

authorHOUSE®

AuthorHouse™
1663 Liberty Drive
Bloomington, IN 47403
www.authorhouse.com
Phone: 833-262-8899

Published by AuthorHouse 11/28/2020

ISBN: 978-1-6655-0933-6 (sc)
ISBN: 978-1-6655-0932-9 (e)

Library of Congress Control Number: 2020923667

Print information available on the last page.

CONTENTS

PREFACE

Dear Reader,

All of our memories carry emotions that are shaped by the mental pictures we paint on the theatre of our mind. However, most people start their day by thinking about the pain of the past and the burdens of yesterday, instead of meditating on the success in small victories and the unlimited possibilites that are in their present moment. Unaware that the images being replayed in their mind are causing subconscious blockages hindering any future progress and expansion, because the person is unconscious to thought and unaware of what they are consciously thinking and feeling. The goal is to live in the now, not tomorrow, then remain aware of what reaction you're having by taking control of how you feel. This is your *"emotional quotient."*

When a person doesn't pay attention to their emotion's their personality trait's begin to alter their life, enslaving them to the emotion's that's associated with bad experiences that leads to poor decision making, and unhealthy behavior that produces bad habits. Our belief system is based upon what we are always assessing or determining to be true about something. However, in order to change your belief system periodically you have to lay all of your cards on the table to reassess what you have once believed about an old concept or idea. What are you constantly thinking about? How often are you rehearsing the images in your mind that cause you to feel the way that you do? It's like taking a step backwards to get that last look in the mirror after getting your best wardrobe on to ensure you are well put together. You believe you are but there are a few reservations lingering around in the space of your mind that need to be silenced. This, oftentimes, persuades a person to alter their thoughts which governs their behavior, and shapes their reality so much that it greatly influences what they have once believed or were taught concerning certain topics such as religion, money, parenting styles, education, marriage and relationships, etc. Causing a person to mirror the environment they were placed in during early childhood. Although a person can have their own belief system in place, it still can be influenced or altered by the opinions of others, external forces, experiences, self-awareness, new found information or higher learning if you keep an open mind. Which means there's space for the *"possibility"* of expanding your consciousness to higher levels of thought so change can take place. Have you ever asked yourself *"What was I thinking?"* or *"Why did I say that?"* I certainly have and to be honest there were times I couldn't even give a good reason or logical explanation as to why I just said or did something. The real reason we say and do things without thinking is because we're conditioned not to think before we speak. The vast majority of people were taught, encouraged and programmed to be as vocal as possible when standing in their own truth. Even if it's at the expense of crushing someones emotions and wounding their spirit. This brings me to the conclusion and the purpose of why you are still alive, and why you have survived all of these karmic lessons and cycles that have come against your divine mind. It's because of the simple fact that you are of significant value to our creator, as well as a precious jewel and a trophy to the almighty God, and you have an assignment in this world to complete. Welcome to Heaven's Master's Classroom 101. Knowing the polarities of good and evil, what is healthy for you and what isn't, to authentically love, forgive, establish healthy boundaries, and how to operate from within instead of without. This is God's main purpose for allowing such hard lesson's that are much needed in order for you to serve the greatest good of all mankind in your life purpose, as you live out your existence in this physical world. Yes, that's right, and the Lord needs your testimony as evidence in the world to those who are walking in ignorance of their true divine nature. Your testimony is going to transform the lives of so many people, and yet bring hope to the hopeless, and encouragement to those who are in the darkest night of despair within their soul. I'm encouraging you to earnestly continue pressing through this night season as the bright rays of the morning sun shines on your pathway to greatness. Allow your inner intelligence system to navigate you through this metamorphosis stage and valley experience regardless of how hard, unbearable, and painful it is. Victory is patiently waiting to embrace you, and your destiny is eager to congratulate you. Remember, one must first become acquainted with the *"creator"* God so one can become better acquainted with oneself. Consistently, learning the universal laws of God, exercising your governmental power and authority, and allowing both components to become the deciding factors that compasses all of your life decisions that will ultimately lead you to amazing experiences you've always imagined. Knowledge is the key that grants you access to opening the portals of abundance of all things in your life when operating in God's system. As you allow these revelations from the spirit to flow freely through the streams of your soul like living water. You will breakthrough to having all that God wants to give you. Spiritual, physical, emotional, and financial blessings will be released to you as soon as you bring stability to your soul. Our soul has to prosper first before we are granted full access to a life of true happiness, health, wealth and abundance. The soul consists of our mind, will, consciousness, emotions, imaginations, memory and perceptions. These are called *"mental faculties"* by which they give us the power and the ability to do something or get something done, causing a person to become powerless if a faculty is lost. After going through my own battfield in the mind, chronic pain, loss and disappointments, I was inspired by the Spirit of the Lord to write this book to awaken the power of positive thinking. It will then teach you how to master your emotions and help you understand the importance of using your God given human imagination that encourages you to dream. This will motivate those who are genuinely connected to you to begin seeking the Lord as it is growing more evident to them that they to are more than a conqueror. Erradicating the root cause of those limiting belief's that once caused them to perceive themselves as victims. Our imagination is merely the architect that builds and structures our mind that allows us to visualize the unknown and bring it into the known which is our physical world. If you can see it in your mind, you can have it in this life because you are broadcasting your thoughts from within that are now being projected into your present reality. Whatever a person feels in their heart and thinks about themselves that's exactly who they will become. People become who they are not who they want to be. As you read this book pray for the mind of Christ and the wisdom of God (II Tim.), have a sound mind and think abundance more than enough until it overflows. Rom. 12:2, *"Be ye transformed by the renewing of your mind."* Realizing that there is absolutely nothing that you can't become nor achieve in this life when you declutter your mind, and bring it back into proper alignment with how God intended for you to think. Comprising these ingredients of wisdom, awareness and understanding that past, present or futuristic experiences will bring you that much closer to you living a life of fulfillment. Because it has lead you to know what to do and what not to do. Giving you a heightened sense of greater discernment and awareness that you are one with the creator of the universe. For no one else is responsible for your life, the thoughts you think, the decisions you make, have made or will make. Liberate yourself from giving the responsibility to others to make your life better or to even make you happy. Humanity must awaken to the self-realization of their God given potential and the infinite power that causes them to create anything as you are an extension of God. This is my prayer for everyone. It is also my desire that you will learn how to turn your dreams into the reality you want, and turn your thoughts into the things you desire by mastering your thoughts and emotions. If God gives us a desire, He knows we have what it takes to become it or He wouldn't have given it to any of us. Whatever it is that you are seeking is seeking you from within. *"Remember true success is when we have found and are effectively functioning in our God given destiny. If not we do not obtain nor do we have the knowledge, spiritual insight or revelation of what true success is."*

Shalom,
Nikki G. MCcray

ACKNOWLEDGEMENTS

First, I would like to thank God for inspiring and anointing me to write this book that will be a vehicle of transformation for you as you learn to apply these principle's, stay consistent and disciplined to alter the course of your destiny and the rest of your life. It is a great honor for the Lord to choose me as one of His earthen vessels to help bring clarity, hope, healing, empowerment and change to those who are imprisoned by unhealthy thoughts. To the person that is constantly swimming in negative feelings while drowning in the sorrow of their roller coaster emotions, desperately wanting to get out of those vicious cycles that has held you hostage for years but not knowing how to, nor having a safe haven to escape to for help and support without judgement. There is hope and healing for you. To those souls who are plagued by distorted belief systems that's been deeply embedded and rooted in your DNA from early child-hood to adult-hood, and to everyone who is paralyzed by the fear of being haunted by recurring negative cycles that seems impossible to break free from. Victory begins when you break up the fallow ground in your heart and evict every thought that doesn't resonate with the truth of God's word, and the beliefs that no longer serve your highest good. Download God's program and implant his divine chip in the heart of your soul so authentic and lasting transformation can take place in all aspects of your life. Allow this book to be a door of change for the sole purpose of helping you get off and stay off of the hamster wheel that has you speeding through life with no forward progression being made. Secondly, I would like to thank my main supporter, prayer partner, mentor and friend in the Lord. A true expression of Christ, His love, patience, compassion for others and forgiveness, My mom Rosa T. Patterson. I love you so much mommy thank you for being a significant part of my journey and life purpose. Step dad Robert E. Patterson Sr., I love you very much. Thank you for supporting and encouraging me in my life's mission for God. Belated Evangelist Rosa Nattiel(Spiritual Mother), Thank you for your prayers, teachings and support. Evangelist Myrtice Powell-Robinson(Spiritual Mother), Thank you for your prayers, teachings and support. Belated Pastor John H. Lawson(Spiritual Father), Pastor Willie Carson(Spiritual Father) and to everyone who walked with me faithfully and to those who fervently interceded for me daily that I would walk into my place in God. To my aunt Evangelist Sandra Thomas, I love you, and I have enjoyed all of our talks about God. A big thank you to two of my dearest friends Diana Rios(Columbia), and Odette Pryce(Jamaica). The best is yet to come and I'm eternally grateful for two angels God has given me. I love both of you amazing women. The world is in our hands so let the travels begin. To my son CJ, thank you for bringing joy and happiness in my life. I love you and I'm very proud of you and to see the man you have become by the hands of the creator is very humbling. Thank you for your unconditional love, prayers, support, sacrifice's, and words of encouragement. To every person that has found themselves acquainted with unhealthy cycles, limiting beliefs and disempowering paradigms through divine revelation and application of the truth of Gods word you will know and walk in God's will, purpose, blessings, and the anointing. Most importantly, the mind will be renewed, prayer will be a daily part of your life, faith will be confessed and positive speech will be born.

CHAPTER ONE

"TRUSTING YOUR INTERNAL GUIDING SYSTEM"

---◆◆◆◆◆---

What is the soul? How relevant is it? How do we change it? Are there signs to alert us that the soul is sick? What narrative are you telling yourself about yourself? What is influencing or governing your decision making? Are you trusting in self? Are you trusting in what you think is right? Or are you trusting in what is never wrong? That would be your GPS within you. Our spirit man is calling us to trust in that still small voice that oftentimes gets ignored and pushed aside for the alter ego. The more you gain insight and clarity on the importance of trusting in your inner man it gives you a clearer understanding that transforming the soul becomes a spiritual compass and catalyst that guides you into true success, purpose, prosperity and your destiny. Let's take this journey together and gain a proper perspective from the mind of God, and allow everything in our core being to become divinely aligned, as we receive all that God has promised us through having our very own *"spiritual awakening"* to who we really are. So we can vibrate on the right frequency, enhancing positive emotions by using visualization techniques (imagination) to manifest the reality we desire to experience from the word of God. Rather than being guided by the logical aspects of a person's five senses. What you can hear, see, taste, touch and feel. Ultimately, you will learn the importance of building healthy pictures in the mind of your imagination and the power of resonating with whatever it is that you are believing God for. Because if you can see it on the blueprint of your mind it's possible for you to experience it in your life now. Coming to the realization and waking up to the truth that the life you want to live is totally up to you. You are the leading actor, writer and producer of your own life not an extra in a movie. If you are not pleased with the life you are currently experiencing at this moment rewrite the script. As the spirit of the living God resides within you, maybe you've asked yourself and God why am I here? You have been placed in this world to expand, evolve, grow, learn, teach, love, leave a legacy when you're gone, and explore the endless possibilites of the infinite power that lives within all of us. Not the limitation's nor the condition's that society has tried to conform us to, as God and His creation are one.

Genesis 1:30; Exodus 46:26, 27 Tells us of the awesomeness of how God breathed the breath of life into man, he became a living ("nephesh"). The soul is the spirit in man that is believed to be seperated from the body and is the source of a persons emotional, spiritual, and his/her moral nature. The conception of right behavior pertaining to our conduct and our character. The teachings we've been exposed to in life determines those standards that seem right or wrong to us. The soul is also thought to be a *"person"* an individual who has rights and obligations. This is the description of *"Soul"* in the New Testament which is Greek means *"psyche"* (psych-to emotionally or mentally prepare oneself). Acts 2:43, At death, the believer enters into the presence of Jesus Christ the author and finisher of our faith. So as believers, God doesn't want us walking in agitation, and uneasiness to men who can only kill our fleshly bodies. Instead, He tells us to fear Him which is able to destroy both soul and body in hell. 2 Tim. 1:7, *"For God has not given us the Spirit of fear but of power, love and that of a sound mind."* We shouldn't trouble ourselves because God has given us assurance. His Death, Burial and Resurrection is our surety of salvation. Secondly, just as a life preserver is needed to keep a person afloat in the water to eliminate drowning. Jesus will be the lifeguard we need Him to be. Always shielding and protecting us from injury because He loves us so deeply and unconditionally. What an awesome God we serve.

Before we came into this physical existence and found fellowship and relationship with the Lord, He was thinking of *"us" "His creation".* I Thes. 4:14 says, *"for if we believe that Jesus died and rose again, even so them also which sleep in Jesus will God bring with Him."* Therefore, be so ever confident in knowing and realizing that it is better to be absent from the body, and to be present with the Lord. We have been created in the image of God serving as a sign and having the ability to do awesome things. God demonstrates His authority over His creation (that's us) through His capacity to bring man into physical existence. Marked by the ability to be greatly creative, imaginative and innovative. In the fall of man, He verbalized and communicated His reluctance to accept the restrictions and boundaries God placed upon Him. Instead man made the effort to become like God. However, due to man's disobedience, it became a natural result. He prevented God's first desired intention for his life. The consequence of man's actions was that he'd become a slave to sin. In order for liberty to come in our life as well as delivering us from the servitude to sin, Jesus had to shed His innocent blood in order to redeem us back to himself. The spirit of lack, doubt, fear, unbelief, condemnation and every other hang up we would encounter is covered in the blood of Jesus. There are numerous excuses for us to stay the way we are. However, we must go forth possessing the promise and succeeding the Lords original purpose intended for mankind. This means becoming co-labourers with the Holy Spirit. As we try to reach for our life to become like God. Did you know that the Bible's general concept doesn't see us as a soul that possesses a body? But it is considered the life principle of the body. When we die in Christ, our soul leaves the body and is freed from physical existence. Although, we may not fully understand the resurrected body we can come to the belief that life after death will include the whole man in the fullness of personal existence.

HOPE

Hope as a Christian is like medicine to the soul. It helps us to go through hard times and gives us strength when we are weak and frail. Jesus gives us confidence and assurance that we will have an expectant end. We don't have to contemplate whether or not we will make it or become successful. It's guaranteed because before the foundations of the world were formed, God predestined us and predetermined our "end from the beginning". Our hope in Jesus Christ is an anchor to our soul. This will allow the faithful Christian to be better able to endure all the fiery darts of the enemy. So you now must believe with expectation of obtaining what is desired. Psalm 146, *"Happy is he that hath the God of Jacob for his help, whose hope is in the Lord his God."* Hope is God's gift to us because it gives us comfort, encouragement and a positive expectation that things are subject to change in the favor of an individual. There isn't a case that is without hope. No not one. Whether it be death, divorce, anxiety, debt, poor health or unhealthy thinking. When negative circumstances occur re-condition the subconscious mind by forcing it to remember that you are significant to the Kingdom of God, and that the enemy only wants to cloud your mind with a bunch of junk, so that you can abort and sabotage your dreams, making it impossible for you to walk into the life you desire, because you are really fighting against yourself and what you believe in your own mind. Purpose is given by God and destiny is up to you and I. Master making good decisions by relying completely on the holy spirit that is ready and willing to aid you in thinking healthy. We overcome any and all subconscious blockages by encouraging ourselves in spending more time with God, and by making sure the environment you're living in will be conducive to Gods presence. One must learn to feed and nurture the garden of the mind by weeding out wrong information (limiting-belief system's) and planting healthy seeds of new information (positive thoughts) in the soil of your heart. Dig up all of those wild roots that no longer serve your life. Now you're in a place to realize that relationship, fellowship and intimacy is what the father longs for and wants. But there first has to be a heightened awareness in the core of your being that you are a spirit that possesses a soul. That has the ability to cause change before change becomes tangible with valid evidences that can be seen by the natural eye or touched with the physical hand.

CHAPTER TWO

"BECOMING A CONSCIOUS CREATOR"

Personally, I would define consciousness as a person having the *"self-awareness"* that you are a little *"god"* not the big *"God"* who has made you a little lower than the angels. And having the understanding of the infinite intelligence that's within you screaming to get out, to expand, spread love and help the world become a better place because you are present in the now, as you have awakened to your higher self. Taking charge of your life and walking in the power God has given you by speaking those things that are not so they can become whatever it is that you've called it. Conscious people take their faith and put it into corresponding action refusing to sit around and wait on the conditions of their life to change because they know who they are. The unconscious person who is oblivious to who they are will always sit at the door of their life waiting for someone to walk by and meet their needs. Are you unaware of who you are? If so, you are living but yet still unconscious on life support because you're dependant on what is external instead of breathing on your own. Meaning, you are not living up to who you are as child of the most high God because you're not trusting the inner man to transform how you think. (Heb. 2:7; Ps. 82:6) We all have been guilty of wrong thinking in our life at some point wouldn't you agree? The reason being for this is because the quality, state or the condition of our mind was in a poor state due to a lack of perception and awareness of who God said we are. Without intimacy with God in His word and in prayer it is impossible for you to become conscious of all the greatness that you are capable of. There is no other solution with lasting results for the transformed soul with a balanced emotional state. As negative thinking takes no real effort to do but on the other hand thinking positive requires effort, discipline and consistency on behalf of anyone who wants to improve the quality of their life. How many times has your ego or that super-ego rained on your parade? Thus, hindering you from the enlightenment needed to interact and connect with God on a deeper level. As for me it felt like a million times I was shaking my head and crying saying *"Lord save my mind."* Help me to do what you said I could and help me to become who you said I am. A small voice at times would say *"you will just trust me"* or I will feel a peace within my spirit I couldn't explain. This is when the realizaton kicked in that I had something on the inside of me that was powerful and loving, and it had been guiding me this entire time even before I learned to trust. Have you ever felt like that? Think about some personal experiences that resonates with you that now causes you to trust your inner man when you normally wouldn't have. When you decide to not trust your inner man it will cause you to confess *"Something told me not to go."* That something has a name and it is the Holy Spirit. Now if you are serious about increasing your level of awareness you can't continue allowing the enemy to keep you stuck in a virus filled program that is not suitable for the life we wish to create and thrive in. If the truth be told there still may be some silent but audible whispers in our mind as we process the mechanics of positive thinking that has yet to be dealt with. How does one master their thinking for the things they do want while overcoming thoughts of what they don't want? There is an art to manifesting the promises of God. It begins in your mind and within the seat of your emotions. Your thoughts are fueled by a series of images that are constantly being played and rehearsed by you over and over again on the cinema of your mind. Which has been derived by the things that has transpired in your life when you were a child, and up until this point causing you to create a belief system that will either benefit your life or destroy it. Why do you think you do the things you do? Or act the way that you do? Most importantly, having a valid understanding that one must become intentional and deliberate when programing their mind for true success is essential in the transformational process of gaining a higher consciousness. God created our mind as an effective, sufficient, working tool to receive whatever we are desiring. The blockages that are delaying the blessings in one's life are those that have negatively influenced man's environment because of unbalanced emotion's, past hurts and trauma's that have not been dealt with. Having a poor perception of self, rejection, loss, abandonment issues, disappointment, and the outcome you wanted that didn't happen just to name a few... I'll let you fill in the blank. The intense battle that's wrestling in your soul right now is requiring that you focus by holding the image of what you are believing God for in your mind. While introducing self to a daily practice of meditation and prayer for the purpose of co-creating every desire and promise of God in your heart to come to fruition easily and effortlessly. Forcing the subconscious mind to focus on whatever you tell it to. Yelp, you can retrain your mind to believe whatever you want it to believe. It's like tirelessly telling a person the truth for the 20th time yet they have convinced themselves that it's a lie, and why it can't possibly be the truth no matter how many times or ways you try and explain it. The life you are currently living right now is evidence of this fact. What internal dialogue are you having with yourself? If you're ready for lasting and positive change in all areas of your life make a committment right now to confront your thoughts and those emotion's that no longer serve you. Discipline yourself to keep your daily routine no matter what. No excuses. Think about some of the world's greatest athlete's that have trained and pushed themselves beyond their own breaking point of what they thought they couldn't do to later find out there was a second wind in them that would give them the outcome of success they had been dreaming about. Now you get to decide on what kind of belief system you want to have. What if God gifted you a blank check from the bank of heaven and told you to write any amount you wanted? Would you struggle and be afraid to write the amount you really wanted? If the answer is yes then you have to do a self-reflection and go within to find out the root cause of your fear. Could it be that you don't feel worthy or good enough? If this is the case go back to that moment in time and confront the pain that has caused you to feel this way, and when you do you're going to realize that the wounded little child in you is responsible for your present dysfunction. Now you've hit a fork in the road. You're at a crossroad to either heal or to keep masking the pain by smiling and serving in false humility. The truth of the matter beautiful souls is that it all begins with a person making a decision about what it is that they really want out of life, and stop meditating on all the things that you don't want. Instead of conforming to the limitation's that life has taught us to believe through circumstances, obstacles, cultural belief's, social and logical thinking *"our ego."* There is no such thing as *"I don't know how to get rid of negative thinking."* Nobody had to teach us how to think wrong. But we have to be taught and be willing to learn how to think positive, as it is a daily war between the will of God and the mind of man. Now that you have been enlightened on how and why you must elevate your consciousness decide to think on a positive note even when things don't go according to plan. Our belief system has also been influenced by our environment and genetic make-up. Accepting the responsibility to educate yourself on how to think positive by uninstalling old patterns and belief's that has not given you the result's you want or deserve will cause your life to take on a successful trajectory. For example maybe as a child you were taught becoming wealthy was out of the question for you. Or maybe you heard your parents speak negative about having large sums of money, or complain and argue about the lack there of. Maybe a leader at your local church told you it's God's will for you not to be wealthy because it's a sign of humility. These are cancerous belief blocker's that you must eliminate from your mind before God's financial blessings can ever be released into your life. Is it possible for a person to say they have the faith to be wealthy but lack the proper belief system that is required to obtain wealth? No. Your spirit has to resonate with whatever you are believing God for or you will not experience it due to your ignorance of this principle. Even if it is your birthright to have it. So if you're believing God for financial freedom you have to feel good in having an abundance of wealth. So the next time you see a wealthy person think positive and not in your old manner of thinking like they must have obtained their wealth by stealing, cheating and lying....What if you were that rich person? Would you want people to pre-judge you and turn their nose up at you because of your material blessings? I'm sure you're getting the point, right? This has to become a daily routine if you want to bring the desired result into your current experience. The things that you allow into your ear gate and eye gate should be soothing, uplifting and positive. Training the mind to think positive thoughts is a matter of that individual first making up their mind they're going to do so. This process will cause you to filter out what you don't want and allow you to visualize or imagine yourself as the successful co-creator that you are. Stick with it even when the going gets tough if you wanna win in the game of life. Don't allow the whispers of doubt and uncertainty cause you to give up to soon. I can tell you from my personal experience when the pressures of life tries to throw you out of the race your breakthrough is at the door. You'll always have to kill a *"Goliath"* before a victory. The size of a battle will determine the size of the blessing. Keep going like the little engine that could. Say, *"I think I can", "I think I can", "I think I can", "I think I can"* and you will. As a child this was one of my favorite stories my mommy use to read to me at night before bed. Little did I know I would literally have to tell myself the same thing when I found myself getting stuck and feeling as if I couldn't take another step. I would repeat this mantra until I got my momentum back. Are you up for the challenge? You can do it. Let me make a suggestion as silly as this may sound to you and as uncomfortable as it may make you feel when doing so. Stand in front of a mirror and tell yourself *"I have changed my mind and belief's about the old concept of happiness, wealth and abundance,"* because I now believe that I am worthy and I am deserving of it no matter who disagrees with me or not. Will you consider the possibilty that there may be more than one solution to a problem? And different ways to handle it for a more productive and peaceful outcome? There will always be more than one way to handle or do anything in life. That's why there are different means of transportation because we get to choose how we will get to the desired destination of our choice. Regardless of what method of transportation a person chooses if New York City was our agreed destination point, we will still arrive in New York, right? Of course that is an undefiable truth. Okay, stay with me family. With chronic practice new habits of healthy thinking will replace old thought patterns and dangerous belief systems. In addition, to this principle remember that your emotions accelerate desires and your thoughts will bring you into the reality you have designed, because you are creating your belief system from this method. While other people are creating a life they don't want from a default system. Not understanding they have the power to change their circumstances. Having an awareness that you are constantly framing your life with your thoughts and emotions whether it be intentional or not will cause a person to not stay in cycles of lack and failure. As you begin to operate from your higher self quantum change will take place. The *"divine spirit"* is the place God expects you to function from. The very moment you left his bosom to live out your time here in the earth realm. Jesus never manifested one miracle by relying on his fleshly nature. There is only one main purpose that God gave us a physical body. That purpose is to merely house the spirit. Our spirit is who we really are and it's our job to get to know ourselves as *"Spirit."* Your earthly name that you have been given is not who you are. As confusing as this may be to you it's true. Although, our earthly name is needed for us to be identified and recognized as we complete our journey while here on earth. It's synonomous to when people ask us who we are and we go rapidly babbling out our entire history. I too have identified who I was by the things I did and what I was blessed to accomplish in my life. Neither of the two has anything to do with who a person is. Personally, I have done this more times than I can remember before the Lord downloaded these revelations to me. A lack of understanding causes us to say things like who our parents are, where we were born, what we do for a living, our accomplishments, our marital status, etc. But none of these things are who we really are. We are spiritual people living in a physical earth realm showing forth our creativity and power as God's expression of Himself. So why are you trying to receive what God said you could have outside of yourself? We were not designed to do so. Jesus manifested Himself in all His mighty acts by tapping into his *"Spirit"* his inward higher self not his flesh. Heb.

5:12, "Wherefore, as by one man entered into the world and death passed upon all men for that all have sinned." By the atonement of Jesus Christ and the shedding of his innocent blood we are free. Rom. 8:1, *"There is no condemnation to them which are in Christ Jesus, who walk not after the flesh, but after the Spirit."* God is a Spirit and we must worship Him in Spirit and in truth. That means everything we know to be true about Him. While remaining in the right attitude, God expects us to acknowledge our sins and confess all of our faults. If we walk in the Spirit we will not fulfill the lust of the flesh. The flesh *"the ego"* will lead you down a dark road to destruction and tell you what you can't do because you have now become self-reliant on your own ability and not that innate God ability. Phil. 4:13 tells us, *"I can do all things through Christ who strengthens me."* This powerful, creative, spirit of the living God is on the inside of us. In which all things exist and are created. Believing is first, now receive what God says about you, who you are in Him and what you can attain with Him. Are you finding yourself saying *"I can't do that"*, *"what will they say"*, are you always comparing yourself to others? Is your mind constantly racing and thinking on carnal issues? Or generational, cultural and social belief systems that has confined you to repeating cycles of failure and defeat? Are you placing negative conclusions about yourself? Or on other's as well? Saying, things like "I can't do this because? Or *"If I was born in the right family"*, *"If people would like me and give me a chance."* Then I can make my dreams come true. This is a constant state of reality you will live in if you choose to believe with this level of thinking. If so, these are some of the symptoms of *"the sick soul."* You have the power to change your thought pattern from these limiting beliefs and disempowering cycles that have invaded your soul not anyone else. Recall when the negative patterns of judgement and reacting began. Although, it's normal for human nature to blame other people for all the unfortunate events that have occured in their life. It is not healthy nor is it benefical to you nor the people you are connected to in any way. Haven't you heard the saying you are what you eat? It's in relation to you will exemplify what you meditate, think and say. The Lord tells us that when we come to him old things are passed away and behold all things have been made new. One may be asking *"what does that mean?"* It means God has a better way of doing what you have been doing all this time, and the results and the reward's are more rewarding than you can imagine. And it's in your best interest to get on the same page as God. Transforming our mind to think like God is the gold treasure chest at the end of the rainbow. Our Heavenly Father wants us to see ourselves as He does because He does. That's why God always calls us what we were not so we can become whatever it is that He called us. Leaving humanity to look for external evidences to match what God has said. Maybe in your reality you're as broke as ever right now but God said *"You are rich in houses and land."* When this revelation is received a person will begin to walk in the awesomeness of his blessings without needing any physical proof. The truth has now been exposed to ignorance causing a person to desire change while going forward in this process to gain a healthy mind. Discipline the mouth to not speak anything anymore that you don't want to come to pass in your life. Get in front of a mirror in your home and declare I'm an overcomer, I'm loved, blessed, abundant, healthy, wealthy, generous, highly favored and powerful. These were some of the affirmation's my mom encouraged me to speak over my life growing up, and at the time I didn't even know that these words were considered *"mantras"* or *"affirmations."* In my early years it was difficult for me to look in the mirror and say nice things to myself. The confidence my mommy gave me while placing her arms around me as she stood with me in front of the mirror telling me I was smart, she was proud of me, I'm beautiful, intelligent and loved. I felt like superwoman. I believed I could do and become anything that I wanted. Although, this may seem a bit weird and difficult at first I encourage you to follow through and don't let the enemy talk you into giving up and giving in to his suggestion. He wants nothing more than to keep you in fear and disbelief. You are on the Brink Of *"Breakthrough."* Now is the time for you to stay diligent, perservere and the ending result will be the spiritual renewal and growth of your mind, speech and spirit. Take this as an opportunity to exercise your faith and tune up your belief system. How do we do that? I'm so glad you asked. We do this by being aware of what we are currently thinking about throughout our day. Faith is what you *"believe"* it's not what you're wishing nor hoping for. The Lord tells us that the just shall live by faith, and not by sight. Learning how to see with our mind *"Our God Given Human Imagination"* is an intrical part of this mental faculty that has been freely gifted to us for the purpose of co-creating. As we desire to experience what we have been dreaming about for so long because we have finally come to the conclusion that we are spiritual people having a physical experience not the other way around. As sons and daughters we live by what we don't see not by what is visible to the natural eye *"Our Five Senses."* Training our Five Senses to operate from the spirit realm is our task. When you think about it the spirit realm is where all things have been created. Just for a moment think about how is it even remotely possible for a blind person to play a piano? They have trained their spiritual sight so that they can see in the physical realm. In the mind of their *"Imagination"* one has created their own physical world which is absolutely normal to them, and abnormal to all of those who have their physical sight but can't wrap their head around the *"possibilty"* of this being done. True sight is seeing the unknown before it manifests in physical form. Did you know that we can't please the Lord without faith? Faith requires you to believe in something before it actually happens and so does fear. Thanking God before the promise knocks on your door or shows up in your mailbox is evidence of an infalliable proof defined as *"faith."* Trust is required, patience is a must have, visualization and positive emotions are key ingredients to laying hold of the promises that are due to you. Now you can't be moved by the circumstances around you just continue waiting patiently until your turn comes. In addition, to knowing that all rushing is not progress meaning people will get saved today and start preaching tomorrow. The majority of us are in a rush not having an ounce of patience to wait for that five course meal, instead we'll settle for a bowl of cereal. Why settle for crumbs when you can own the entire company? Isn't it wise for us to allow the Lord to use our not enough to become more than enough? Have you ever rushed to a department store to buy your favorite piece of merchandise one day and then the next week you come too learn the item you purchased has now been discounted at half price off? Now you're digging to find the receipt so you can take it back to the store and get the discount? God is trying to tell you/us something. Sounds comical but that's what happens when we can't wait. When you can't get your hands on what you want right now you'll turn into a character you didn't even know was inside of you. It only takes two loaves of bread and five fish to feed a multitude of people with fragments left over. This requires *"time"* and it's a *"process."* While in the process you're going to have to refrain from murmuring and complaining about your living situations because that's what you have built. We all are living in the houses we have built and constructed. What you think about you attract. Like attracts like. Think about a magnet and how it attracts other properties of magnetism, such as attracting other iron-containing objects in an external magnetic field and so does your thoughts. Although, the magnetic field is invisible it's still responsible for attracting or repelling materials. Hopefully, you are gaining an understanding of how much power the thoughts you think hold. This is where our transformation begins by fine tuning and aligning our consciousness with that of the mind of God. So the life you're presently exisiting in at this moment is your reality. The one you created and designed straight out of your own head and free will. A person can't talk positive and think negative in hopes to receiving anything from God. What you are desiring must resonate with your belief system or what you want will not come to pass. That's what it means to be double-minded and it's a waste of time and energy. Deprogram the old way of thinking by removing those old viruses (unhealthy thought patterns) that's in your head that has caused you to fail and install a new program *"the word of God."* It's the choices that we make right now that will shape our tomorrow. The truth's and principles that God exposes us to is our responsibility as we are held accountable for the truth that we hear. Renew your mind with the word of the Lord daily. Prov. 16:3 says, *"commit to the Lord whatever you do, and your plans will prosper and succeed."* Always keep in mind that whatever resources you need to win in life is in our Lord and Savior Jesus Christ. This same power resides within you. There is no need to look for anything externally when you have it all internally. Go within and not without. A healthy life starts by a person looking within themselves. Now go for it! Block out everything and everyone that will hinder your transformation process. Just be mindful that people will always have something negative to say in hopes of convincing you not to change for the greatest good that will bring light to all mankind. Constantly, overshadowing you with their internal insecurities, fears and inferiorities due to a lack of courage that they don't have. When an individual becomes aware of you trying to reach another realm in God, grow spiritually or even strive to become the best in your field in the corporate world. Fiery darts are going to come out to shut you down. I call people like this as having a *"crab bucket mentality."* They don't want to go higher in the Lord and they don't want you to go higher either. Let the Lord sanctify and seperate you from the *"goats."* We are the temple of God so this means we do not own ourselves. Our entire being belongs to God, He has paid the ultimate price for us. We were created in the image of God to work in *"The Kingdom of God."* It's time for us as saints of the most high God to go forth discipling, ministering, witnessing, and bringing as many souls to the Lord as possible. We must be swift in being about our Father's business and not our own. There is no time for us to be passive and complacent. We must get out of these comfort zones we are in. Many of us stay in this place because it's the land of familiarity and we don't have the courage to step out on faith and launch into the deep in a place we have never been in. It's scary to build a business for the first time. You just have to double tie your shoe laces and keep building, and not concern yourself with all the details. Like where are the resources going to come from? Who will I get to help me? What if I fail at this? Failing at something is learning how to do it better the next time. If you don't give it a try then you fail. So leave every intricate detail for God to sort out as only he can do. Remember how you tried to be God? And it only frustrated you because you ended right back at the starting point yet again. A place called *"nowhere"* If you want to see different things come to pass in your life, you have to do what you have never done before. This is the only way new results can be birthed in our lives. There's a harvest in the world longing for laborers to come and rescue them. God allows circumstances to come about in our life to shape us, mold us, redefine us and purify us for His purpose. So get out there and open up your mouth and declare the word of the Lord. By our faith (what you believe) we can do all things through the blood of Jesus. Close the door to the enemy by denying Him access to your mind ensuring that you will not be subjected to his satanic attacks any longer. If the enemy can get in your head, he then can control how you think and how you feel. Now his suggestions have taken root in your heart and you're working for him. Being totally governed and ruled by him. God is our boss and He gives us instructions and directions. God will revolutionize our life if we will allow Him to. As we would take the time to exercise to keep our bodies physically fit we need to take time out for God in his word. To keep our spirit man healthy, learn to love the word of God, admire it, digest it deep within your heart. Without the word of God we will have no guidance nor peace. God has great things in store for those who love Him. How can one say I love God and hate their neighbor? Pray and intercede for others before yourself. Whatever we make happen for others God will make happen for us. So what's missing, lacking or broken in your life the anointing will put it in it's rightful place. God has given his people recompense a blood covenant of peace, prosperity, blessings and healing. Our God is a covenant keeping God, He will not remove it because He is *"TRUE"* and *"FAITHFUL."* Be strong in the Lord and in the power of His might knowing that He is faithful in all of His promises. That's why it's so important and beneficial for us to live a life perfect (completeness) and upright before Him. Prov. 3:5-6, tells us to *"trust in the Lord and lean not to your own understanding. In all thy ways, acknowledge the Lord and He will direct your paths."* Allow the spirit of the Lord to renew your mind. Look over your shoulders and say *"That's in the past now."* Look in front of you and declare *"This is where my future is and I will never look back or meditate on my past again."* If you don't have a prayer life get one because this is how we communicate with God. You have to put the work in yourself if you want a better life. God is not going to force you to do anything you don't want to do because you have a *"free will."* He has given you the ability to decide and to choose. We are God's highest creation over everything He created because we have been made in His likeness and in His image. Knowing the difference between good and evil. Prayer simply equals success in mastering positive thinking and overcoming negative cycles of failure, because when a person is in true prayer mode they vibrate on a high frequency of positive emotions. Allowing everyone they come in contact with to feel that positive energy. Energy cannot be destroyed and it moves like an ocean. This is what The Law Of Perpetual Transmutation means everything is always moving. Haven't you ever stepped in a room full of people and it felt weird making you a bit uncomfortable? That's because the energy of those individuals vibrated on a level of negative emotion in that space. And you didn't vibrate on their frequency (negative energy/emotion). Instead the frequency you are vibrating on is (positive energy/emotion). When we become a House of Prayer, we stay in a state of gratitude cooperating with the spirit of God within ourselves that enables us to become powerful co-creators. Being led by our internal gps. When you are not creating the reality that God has said that you could you will experience fear, doubt then worry shows up to only encourage you to suppress your negative emotions and feelings. This is very unhealthy to do because it only causes you to feel anxious, depressed and oppressed causing the physical body to break down through sicknenss and disease, because there is so much dissatisfaction in your soul and you're going to have to learn how to express how you feel. Whether it's good or bad, the mind can be trained to remain in a state of peace and serenity. The life of a person involving daily prayer will result in good success and a sense of contentment. Stay plugged in to God. He is our life support so stay connected. When we pray out of the sincerity of our heart God will move on our behalf. Healing in our mind, emotions, perceptions are all on the wings of the Holy Spirit. Confess all ill-thinking, bitterness, and unforgiveness to the Lord so he can assist you. Dump all your garbage it's dead weight and it's only weighing you down so you won't walk in victory. You can't reach your full potential in life if you are going to hold on to those past hurts, setbacks, failures, limiting belief systems and disappointments. Jesus went to the cross, bled and died for situations just as this. Nothing should be more important in our life than transforming our minds and lives to the way that God has told us in His word. Renewing the way we think by installing God's program which is His word has to be a daily routine. Keep the divine chip in your mind. We must be diligent, cultivate our hearts and be willing to do what God has told us to in His word. When I think of Jesus hanging on a cross after being beaten, scourged, spit on, mocked, made fun of and pierced in his side I say to myself *"Yes Lord."* I can say yes with ease and not have to think twice about it. God has done so much for us and the least we can do is say yes. It is my prayer that the Lord will give you a heart for the things that concern the Kingdom of Heaven. All of our blessings, deliverances and miracles are only going to come about when we walk in total obedience and submission to him. There's no way around it. We have to walk through the front door which is Jesus. If we try to come in any other way you will not be permitted to enter. It's like the witches and warlocks using their magic, spells, potion's and objects to enter into the spirit realm to which they haven't been given authority nor granted permission to enter. They're a thief to God they snuck in through the back door. Everything we have belongs to God and everything you are looking to do or ever accomplish is in the Lord. Don't let the negativity of other people rub off on you nor affect you. It's important that you choose to magnify the awesomeness of those good things in your life. Focus on positive experiences and never the negative experiences. Learn from it, grow and move forward. Faith always anchors us to become victorious in our life regardless of what the situation looks like. There is no point in magnifying what is wrong in your life so start focusing on what it feels like to be that person you've always imagined you could be. God didn't give us suggestion! God gave us His *"word"* His *"promise"* and man can't alter what He has spoken. The laws are God made and not man made. God has commanded us to go into all the earth as ambassadors proclaiming the good news. Teaching and training people who are walking in darkness to know that there is a better and more excellent way. God is asking *"Can I count on you to get yourself together so you can become a mirror to others and help them find the missing pieces to the puzzle in their own life?"* God has fought every fight that we will ever have to face. God's waiting on you. When He created us, He equipped us for the job. Our problem sometimes is that we really don't believe we're who God says we are. Through this book I earnestly pray that the towers of doubt, inadequacy, disempowering belief's and negative cycles that you've built will be torn down by the transformation of God's belief system. As light is like wisdom we need knowledge to successfully operate in the things of God. So when stress arises in your life and conditions go beyond your limitation's stay committed to God. Persecution comes as a mere distraction to take your focus off of God and to overwhelm you with frustration after frustration in hopes of you giving up. Keep the attitude of faith and expectancy no matter what is taking place around you. Use your will power to hold the image of the promise in your mind while you go through the storms of life. God wants to help us because we're His children and he loves us. So let him do it. Think about what lengths a natural parent will go through to keep their child safe. There's no barrier that will hinder nor prevent me from getting to my son! So trusting (The Law Of Surrender) Him in hard times proves to God that we believe in Him and expect our outcome to be victorious. God wants to do the impossible and the extraordinary in our life. He wants us to live with confidence and assurance in His word so that we can enjoy the abundant life that He promised. Don't have a bitter attitude have a positive attitude knowing that you have the favor of God in your life. Wake up every day expecting Gods favor and open up your mouth and declare it. You can expect God to assist you with advantages and preferential treatment. Did you know that God looks at all of our failures, disappointments, missed opportunities as a vehicle to impart miracles in our life? God took in account every act of our disobedience and weaved it into His will. He knew how hard headed and rebellious we would be but when you are chosen for real all things will work for your good and God will be glorified. So don't try and get out of the process. It's useless because I can tell you from my own personal experiences you will end right back in the fiery furnace. Only prolonging your blessing. Guess what? You are still going to do what He told you to do from the very beginning so save yourself some heartache and pain and just obey God the first time. Never let the chaos and pain of life deter you and cloud your mind with a bunch of junk. Don't ever let people bury your dream! That's why it's important that we become selective in the company we keep yet keeping our goals and plans to ourselves. It can be quite dangerous to share your dreams with family and friends. Joseph, was our example as to why it's a good idea to keep our mouth shut even if we want to tell the world what God said to us and what He showed us. Now put your hand on your mouth and say *"Lord help me learn to keep my mouth shut."* I definitely had to learn this because it's very exciting when God reveals things to you. It makes you want to share it but it's a mistake. People sometimes won't be excited for you and share the same positive emotion as you. And like myself you feel bad now because you just knew your friend/family member would be happy for you instead they're negative to you about all that good news you've just shared with them or they're not even moved by your theatrics, poking doubt into all your faith and positive emotions. Everyone that says they're for you aren't. So when your confidants sense there's a change in you, and when you start rebuking them from speaking negative, and from bringing you gossip they will begin to walk away. Let them and don't pray fake people back into your life. Wave goodbye to all of them. Time is of the essence and it's been given to us by God to invest wisely and not to waste on the people who don't want to do anything except but make a mess of your life. However, you do want to know if there's a *"Judas"* or *"Satan"* walking with you so you can know what category to put these people in. God doesn't show us the heart of people so we can be ugly to them. He shows us so we can discern between *"good"* and *"evil"* so we don't continue investing where there will be no return. It doesn't matter how anointed, gifted or talented you are discernment and faith are by far the most important components to you as a believer. Wait! Don't get discouraged because God knows what's best for you. All of our life choices up until this point is undeniable evidence of this fact. Those of us who succeed are those who endure trials. Be accepting to the chastening of the Lord because he knows what's best. It's time for us as children of God to possess our inheritance and walk into our Canaan. Without clothing our mind with fear because there's *"giants"* in the land that is flowing with milk and honey. Imagine the enemy already defeated because he is. The true battle is what you're telling yourself. Get your weapons out and fight. The Lord is telling us to ARISE! We need to grow up and get rid of the spirit of inadequacy. Through God we are called to be ministers releasing the Holy Spirit. We need to always be mindful of what we utter because when we speak negative words we open the door to the enemy and when we speak positive words we close the door to the enemy. How long will you carry the bondage and slave mentality? I encourage you to think like and act like the mighty men and women of God that you are. That means you don't have to try and become successful you already are. One must master *"The Art Of Acting As If"* before it ever comes into physical existence. It reminds me when I was in elementary school and if the teacher saw you staring into space daydreaming (playing with your imagination) you were told to put your thinking cap on and focus on the real world. You see these negative paradigms we've been exposed to have to be uninstalled and rebooted with new information. From the tallest skyscraper building to the most gorgeous piece of art it was first created out of someone's imagination, then into our physical world. They daydreamed about it in their mind until they pictured every detail that would be pleasing to them, and to those who would benefit from the mastermind of their thoughts. New information will come to you through new experiences, educating yourself, skill and application. A person's imagination is where their mental faculties (will, imaginations, perception's etc.) and creative juices shape and frame the life they want to have. Because they've learned the importance of turning positive thoughts into the things they want and enjoying the benefits of cooperating with their own imagination. Great people like Jesus Christ, Nicola Telsa, Steve Jobs, Thomas Edison, Bob Proctor, The Wright Brothers and Napolean Hill just to name a few tapped into something that changed their life and the core of history. Yes, your *"God Given Human- Imagination."* How do you perceive yourself? What is the self image that you have of yourself in your mind? It's time that you tear down and destroy your strongholds and vision yourself as the anointed one and his anointing does. Next step is to make a conscious decision to believe the report of the Lord and build your life on the rock (foundation of Jesus Christ). Which is the word of God..........A strong and firm foundation. The enemy is definitely doing his job and we need not be alarmed at him, instead we need to be diligent, vigilant, sober and persistent in resisting him instead of crying and feeling sorry for ourselves. That's what the enemy wants you to do. If he can get you in a place of self-pity he can cripple and paralyze you. Strengthen yourself...It's either fight or flight! Faith or Fear! Sink or Swin! Satan always brings suggestions to our mind just like he did Eve. *"Did God really say?"* That's what he is asking us today. The enemy is still using the same pick up lines he has always used but it doesn't have to work on you. God tells us that the enemy is the father of lies so let every man be a liar and let God be true. If we know all of this what is our problem? We're not being conscious and aware of what we're thinking about on a day to day basis, which is due to ignorance. People don't think their life is the way that it is because of their thoughts, they believe some person or an unfortunate circumstance that has happened to them is the main reason why their life is the way that is. This doesn't mean the bad things that has happened to us hasn't caused a bit of collateral damage. It means we can't allow these negative experiences to guide the course of our entire life. If you want to change the direction that the course of your life is taking then change the way you think, and what you believe about whatever it is that you desire to change. Change what you believe, what you're thinking, and feeling because it's causing your life to be either out of order or in alignment with who God created you to be. It's quite simple to identify or know which state you're in because you're going to either feel a great deal of dissatisfaction, discontentment or you'll experience emotion's of satisfaction and contentment. The next time a negative thought, feeling or emotion tries to invade your inner man it won't be able to get in because you are so full of positive energy. Even your circumstances has to bow down to the name of our Lord Jesus Christ. So what you are going through is purposeful and profitable to your destiny so grin and bear it. Trust in the Lord and lean not to your own understanding. He is going to bring you out refined and purified. First, God has to show us how nasty, arrogant, hateful, rude, jealous and envious we are before we can receive what He has for us. Is this what you want to broadcast to the world? And is this how you want the people in your life to see you? Is this how you want to be viewed on the movie screen of your life? How will you use the influence that God has given you? This is not the time to get discouraged. However, it is time to pray and ask God to help you with you, and reveal to you the root cause of your problem. If you want to fix the problem find the root cause of a thing and stop putting a bandaid on it. This is a temporary fix and how many temporary fixes have we all been through that didn't fix us? We medicated the symptom instead of healing the condition's of our soul. It's during trying times like these that the enemy will come and try to discourage you, make you feel guilty and make you feel like you're not good enough because he doesn't want you to move forward. You have to be able to stand in a mirror and tell yourself you are good enough because you really are good enough. Say it until you begin to believe it and when those positive emotions vibrate on that frequency positive change is occuring. That's why you need to hang in there and focus on where you are going. Keep your vision alive and don't let the enemy abort your dream. Salvation is our gift from God and sin is God's dilemma. There's no need to panic and let go of the the spirit of fear and sadness. Cast all your cares upon the Lord because He cares for you. Get out of the drivers seat. God is in control so surrender your will and desires totally to Him. It's absolutely okay to be vulnerable to God. His plans for your life are much more fullfiling than your plans could ever be. It's so essential that we conquer the battle in our soul and overcome these negative cycles because it's the key to us being successful in all things. Being conscious of what you are thinking, feeling, saying and perceiving are the main ingredients to your breakthrough and living the life you really want to live. Having spiritual ears, being synchronized to the frequency of God makes it possible so you can receive His direction, deliverance to destroy demonic anchors in your soul, seeds of disempowerment, unhealthy belief systems and now you're ready to embark on a life of health, oneness and wholeness due to you being properly aligned with God creating a healthy soul, and an amazing life because you are the master builder and co-creator of it.

CHAPTER THREE

"BUILDING A GOOD SUPPORT SYSTEM"

By surrounding yourself with the right people when you're in the drought of your life will cause your confidence level and your hope to be renewed. While engaging in a toxic circle of people will cause you to travel the road to doom (Psalm 1). Do you have an *"inner circle?"* Jesus sure did and so should you and I. Your social circle should always include the people you trust the most and who can give you proper guidance. These may include parents, coaches, mentors, family members, friends, and etc. This is exactly what successful people do. Everything in life is about equal *"give* and *take"* not *"push"* and *"pull"*. Like the words of Jesus, *"Treat people like you want them to treat you."* How do you relate to other people? Think about if you are supportive to other people or not? Are you offering what you can to others? While making it crystal clear to everyone that will listen to you that you have needs as well, and there will not be continuous withdrawals from your life without equal deposits being made. Why is it even important to develop a strong support system? Because it promotes positive changes in the different ways we conduct our lives that benefits our emotional and physical well being. Secondly, it allows us to stay connected while creating meaningful relationships. And when you can be honest it's a sign and an indicator that when you admit you need help you show forth great strength and not weakness. The Son of God asked His own disciples to pray for Him in The Garden Of Gethsemane. Was this a sign of weakness? No, not at all, what courage and strength did Jesus display, letting us know that we will go through seasons of great despair, and we will need those closest during our midnight agony. The spirit is always willing but it's the flesh that is weak. However, some may walk away or fall asleep on you during your darkest night season. Jesus looked at His fellow disciples as members of His family and His friends. Are you calling your enemies friends and perceiving a true God given friend an enemy? A true enemy will always oppose the will of God for your life, and fertilize the parts of you that God has been trying to bury. God never intended for you to go through anything alone but the enemy sure did. Have you ever asked yourself why? It's a tactic to get you alone so he can conform you to his ways of thinking. Surround yourself with positive people who are team players. God has definitely assigned an army of warriors to aid you in winning every battle that has the audacity to try and consume you by betrayal, rejection, sickness, etc. Understand that God said *"No weapon formed against you shall prosper"* (Rom. 8:28). He's right in the midst of the trial with you. But do you believe Him? You have to believe Him so you can stop stumbling your way through life. The battle isn't given to the one who is the strongest nor the swiftest, but only to that person who can *"endure"* all the way to the end of the finish line. Listen family, just because you can't physically touch what God told you was yours yet doesn't mean it's not yours. It means you have to make the necessary adjustments in your life and stretch yourself like David, when he pulled back and stretched his sling shot with a rock in it to slay *"Goliath."* Get the enemy out of your head. Tell yourself I'm going to accomplish everything God said I would. I will do everything God said I could. I will no longer be manipulated by the distractions of the enemy and abort my destiny. No Way! I'm a fighter and I'm a winner. Don't allow your issues and insecurities to cause you to disconnect with other people. Because so many people feel like their brokenness and indiscretion's disqualifies them from experiencing God's favor. These are the very things that causes the horn of oil to be poured upon us to be used by God and bring Him glory. Now you're constantly having this conversation with God telling Him everything that's wrong with you as if He doesn't already know. He already know's how many strands of hair are on your head remember. Can you imagine how much better your life would be if you would just get the courage and command the enemy in Jesus name to move out of your way? Some people are easily susceptible in allowing the enemy to lead them astray because they're led by their emotions and their flesh all the time. Doing and giving the flesh anything and everything that it wants. Then complaining about how bad things are in which they are responsible for creating by thinking it, feeling it and voicing it.

In itself, flesh is morally non-supportive but is subject to worsen and is inevitably in relationship with death. Despite it's weakness our flesh is needed for human existence. God in His supremacy chose to be the vessel and manifested himself in his son Jesus (flesh). The Lord wants us to train our flesh and bring it under control in order to preserve our spirit. As we would place sugar on fruit to preserve it and prevent it from spoilage.

Gal. 5:16 says, *"I say then walk in the Spirit, and ye shall not fulfill the lusts of the flesh."* The spiritual things of God are life and peace. If we walk under divine direction of the Holy Spirit we will be delivered from selfish lusts. When God saved us he gave us an absolute new life and a new way of thinking so we can receive what is already ours. The Christian can conquer the battlefield in the mind and have continual victory by walking in alignment with the Holy Spirit, and by casting down negative patterns of thinking that we have been exposed to when Adam and Eve fell in the Garden of Eden. Yes, our garbage can thinking came about when Adam and Eve disobeyed God and ate from the tree of knowledge of good and evil. Now there's a war going on in your head that is opposing what God told you to do and what not to do. Secondly, you have to hold yourself accountable and keep your thoughts in sync and in proper alignment with the word of God. Push through the pain, silence the contrary voice that is at odds with what your spirit is saying, and stop allowing the flesh to have total and complete control of your life. If a person thinks wrong their life will end bad. So if you want to have a healthy life you must have a healthy mind. This is the underlying problem to the frustrations that people are experiencing today. As a man thinketh in his heart so is he. Whoever you are right now is what you've imagined and thought within yourself that you are. We are what we think and feel. In the process of transforming the pattern of your thinking from carnality to spirituality it is going to take more than your will power. Jesus has already given every person in this world all the necessary tools they will need to become a winner in life. Realize that you already have the tools you need to do a quantum shift in your thinking now it's time for you to pick them up and use them. Find scriptures, write them down, memorize them and speak them over the areas in your life that you desire to see a change in. What good is it to know what you have and never apply what you know? That is called ignorance. Wisdom is knowing what you have then applying it. Faith is believing it with a supportive action because faith without works is dead. Belief requires a response. When you continually keep your eyes and thoughts fixated on the word of God a greater self concept of yourself will be developed and you'll be less likely to engage in destructive behaviors, negative patterns of thinking (Old Paradigms) and habitual habits that has the potential to destroy your life. Now you're tapping into your true self the spiritual being that has been given power and authority over everything. What images do you have of yourself in your mind? Are you allowing negative thoughts to stick around in your mind? Or are you kicking them out? The thoughts that you have allowed to be planted and to grow in the field of your mind is what's causing your life to be shipwrecked. How often are you rehearsing the pains of your past on a daily basis? If this is what you're doing you are reliving your past instead of learning lessons from it and moving forward. Stop telling the same story over and over again because this makes it more difficult for you to change the old belief system to a new and healthier one that will serve your life for the better. What and who has influenced your thinking? Our mind responds to pictures. Re-create positive thoughts, images and crucify negative images that are trying to over power your vision, perception, beliefs and self-esteem. This is done through the power of prayer, mediation, daily affirmations and by using the power of your God given human imagination. After applying these kingdom's principles consistently, you will begin to see small miracles take place in your life. As a farmer sows a seed in the ground to reap a harvest he or she knows it takes time for the fruit to produce. So it shall be for you. Continue reconditioning your mind by replacing every negative image with a positive thought, emotion, concept or idea. I can tell you from my own personal experience it's going to be extremely difficult for you think unhealthy. You've now positioned yourself to become everything that God already said you are. There is no longer a battle going on between the spirit and the flesh. Remember the images in your mind will reproduce whatever you are thinking and meditating on whether it is negative or positive. The Laws of God governs the entire universe and one of the reasons people are failing in life is due to the ignorance of not knowing how to operate the principles of God. What are the Universal Laws of God you may be asking? It's how God expects us to conduct our lives through the system he has put in place. Not by the systems, methods or beliefs the world has tried to conform you to. Begin by reading the book of Genesis. A person's emotions and feelings are going to accelerate the process of manifesting the desired outcome in your life. Simply thinking about what you want isn't enough to bring it into your reality. When tough times visit your present circumstances standing firm in your faith and focusing on the promise and not the problem that you can physically see is the only alternative to your victory. Decide right now to let every hurt and offense take the next flight out of your life that no longer serves you and allow the sweet, loving Holy Spirit come in, and do whatever He needs to do to get you functioning like you were pre-ordained to before the earth was created. While putting off the old man---that means the old self has to die. Go ahead and have your funeral, cry, have your fits and your temper tantrum's. It's a done deal. Say ashes to ashes and dust to dust. Now wipe your tears and wash your face, and start smiling and rejoicing your new beginning is just beginning. Praise the Lord! Bringing all those unhealthy thoughts, belief's, desires, motives and behaviors under subjection to the Holy Spirit and by the power of God is your focus now right? This is going to bring so much peace in your life when you receive and embrace this revelation. There were times in my own personal life as a *"Christian"* I was struggling with myself. Thank you Lord for your mercy. I was a worshipper, faithful to the Lord, living a life of holiness, giving, tithing, sowing seeds in other peoples lives. I had a prayer life but was not living the fullness of the abundant life God said I would. My mind needed to be transformed and renewed. Did you know that after you make a decision to come to Jesus that's not all you need to do? You have the responsibilty of dealing with your own traumatized soul that is against God. Yes, you and not anyone else. The journey that a person is on is their personal journey. Can another run a race for you then win and give you the prize? Only the person who runs and completes their race will receive the crown of life. How long have people been in the church and still find themselves struggling with the same old issues that has plaqued their life for years? Not knowing the reason for those unhealthy recurrences is due to a lack of knowledge in using the keys of the kingdom God left for us in his word. Like a precious pearl that's been hidden from an intruder one must seek to find the treasures in the word of God.

One summer, I injured my left wrist and as a result of that I had to wear a hard, monster cast for approximately 7 weeks. I said within myself *"OK after this I can go about my business and continue my life."* Boy, I was so wrong!... What was about to take place in my life would challenge me personally, physically, emotionally and spiritually. I began experiencing burning, aching pain in my hand. At times my hand would become mottled and blue, extremely cold and sensitive to any touch and weather. The pain was absolutely unbearable and excruciating at times that my mind began to race and take trips. *"This was not suppose to be happening,"* I said to myself. My doctor referred me to have physical and occupational therapy for months, but this was unsuccessful and made the condition and symptoms in my hand hurt worse. This left me upset, confused and frustrated because no one seemed to know what was wrong.

Eventually, during one office visit, my doctor gave me a brochure on *"RSD", "CRPS I AND CRPS II",* and said I was being referred to a specialist. After reading that brochure on this illness I was devastated, crushed, frustrated and to be totally honest not hopeful. My carnal self was in full force and my main focus was looking at how devastating this nerve condition was not that by the stripes of Jesus I was already healed. I walked out of that office, got myself in my car and while driving home I could hear that doctor say there is no cure!!! However, there are different medications, surgical procedures, and other medical modalities we can attempt in decreasing your pain and sensitivity level. This sounded like a death sentence to me. I didn't want to hear that's all that we will be able to do. I didn't want to think of how I would suffer with this *"FOREVER."* I know this probably seems hard to believe coming from a born again believer who loves the Lord but it's true. RSD (Reflex Sympathetic Dystrophy Syndrome) and I became very close. I became depressed, sleep deprived, hopeless, sad, at times being up 24 hours without sleep. And I isolated myself wanting to be alone. This is exactly what the enemy wanted. He wanted me alone so he could target my strength, paralyze my thinking, manipulate my weakness and suffering against me to literally destroy my life, so I would abort my dream and destiny. There were times that I didn't want to keep going. I wanted to just throw the towel in and quit. This is his plan for all humanity so don't be ignorant of his devices. Don't succumb to the voice, temptations, frustrations and negative forces of the enemy. My life had changed drastically. Even my independence suffered greatly. My self-esteem had fallen and now my mommy had to refocus her role in my life as my caregiver and surrogate mother for my son. Thank God for a God fearing, faith walking, word declaring, prayer warrior woman of God *"My Mommy."* What a powerful and solid support system I had then and continue to have in my mother today. Without it, I don't think I would be here today. I was raised to be independent and productive so this trial was a big slap in my face. A huge struggle and disappointment.

My mommy never complained, never got tired of being there, she always prayed for me, spoke the word of God over me and I don't know how many times she held me in her arms and cried with me placing her soft hands on my teared face, wiping rain drop tears away while looking me in my eyes to tell me yet again who I am in Christ, and how I would come out of this storm greater, more anointed for the Lord to help his people. These were some of the most trying times of my life and the enemy knew it. I felt like job quite often. In faith this minute and questioning my salvation and sanity the next. The attacks of the enemy worsened because he sensed my weakness and vulnerability then he took advantage of me while I was in a low place. I began to doubt and accept the lies and suggestions of the enemy as maybe some of you have. I believed that God could heal me but the enemy had my mind so perplexed that I began to say *"God is not going to heal me, face it, accept it and move on."* I was in the fight for my life as some of you are right now as you are reading this book. But remember we are overcomers by the blood of the Lamb and by the words of our testimony. Daily I was struggling to bring all of the enemies lies and thoughts under control by the power of God. Was this easy? Not at all! The more I persevered in the word of God, and prayed the stronger my faith and perceptions of the love and power of God became. The Lord began to transform me and do a greater work from within me. My desire to win in life was reborn again causing my faith to be renewed. Isn't it funny how God will allow pain and distress to perfect us into His glorious image. After all, the Father said it pleased Him to bruise His only son *"Jesus"* my God.

Whatever you do, I strongly encourage you not to despise nor resent God because this is where your strong anointing gets birthed. Straight out of all those hard, painful, detestable and hurtful things you have been through. Until we start weeping about how our generation is living and start fasting about it God will not quickly run to our rescue. The Lord is trying to get his people beyond their selfish lusts, wants, desires, and start desiring what he desires. Yes, I know we have been hearing this down through the years and it's time to stop being fake, phony, religious and flaky Chrisitans. You have a real adversary who is not playing games about destroying your life. Some people are wasting time, their life and mere opportunities by patty caking with the devil. As long as the enemy can keep people waring against their desire and faithfulness to be totally, completely governed, ruled by The Spirit of God, he is extremely beside himself. The enemy doesn't want us to walk in obedience to God because he knows when we do, his camp is doomed causing every plan and diabolical assignment that he has devised for the destruction of your life to be canceled. Every person must come to the point in their own life and say okay I know I want to be blessed by God. So I don't have a choice whether or not I will obey Him. When a person is led by the spirit of God this is how they pray. This is a decision you must make if you are ever going to get to your desired place "your destiny". When you think about it and ask yourself this question isn't it the absolute truth? Do you know how much damage you can do to the enemy? Do you know how successful you will be when you receive this revelation? There will be nothing that you set your hands to do that it won't prosper. Of course this still means that you will face and encounter adversity but all things will work for your good "Romans 8:28."

To be honest, there was a time in my life where I was afraid to surrender everything to God and give Him complete and total control. Why? Because God just might ask me to give up something dear to me and maybe I wouldn't be ready to give it up. Having the mindset that God wants us to have is something you must work toward. Loving what God loves and hating sin. Even while you're in the midst of a storm being able to say God loves me and if He decides something/someone isn't right for me--so be it. If He thinks it will draw us away from Him or if He sees it will be harmful to our life, give God permission to remove it. When it's all said and done if you don't you're going to wish it was gone. God is going to allow so much trouble on that situation because He's a jealous God. I'm going to trust God in His decision making even if I don't fully understand, if I don't agree with it or if I don't think it's fair or not. He is my father and He desires to see me blessed, whole, healthy and complete. I'm going to humble myself before Him and commit my ways to Him. This is the best attitude to have because God knows the end from the beginning and we at times are looking at the present moment and that's just not going to do it in The Kingdom of God. If there is anybody that we can trust and have total confidence in, it's God. When the tests and opportunities make an appearance in your life because they both will, allow the Spirit of the Lord to direct and lead you even if it's in an unfamiliar surrounding. In the end, you will be glad that you did.

Promotion comes when a test has been passed and life lessons of betrayal have been learned. After this Kingdom Principle is mastered, we won't be so eager to get ourselves in alot of mess. Why? Because we will be trusting and submissive to the Father knowing we don't want to go back to bondage. The enemy wants us to view God as if we can't trust Him. As if He won't hold his end of the deal. Satan has always tried to smear Gods name by painting a negative image of Him in our mind as if God's a liar. The image that satan has shown you believe Him. You shall know the tree by the fruit it bears. Don't always pay attention to what people are saying watch what they do as well. This is so important but overlooked. Being aware of the tactics of the devil is where you get to decide whether you live or die, keep going or give up. God said He wouldn't have us to be ignorant of the enemies devices. That's why it is so essential that we study the word of God gaining the knowledge that's needed to live a victorious life. So we can know who He is, what He requires of us, and learn the characteristics of Him who has given us all power and dominion. If you want to defeat your opponent you have to study his strength's and weaknesses. The Lord is longing for us to get sincere, search our motives and pursue a personal relationship with him. He wants us to talk to Him on a daily basis and tell Him how much we love Him, and how awesome we think He is. Get intimate with God through His word, through prayer, stay connected and having the only motive of pleasing Him, so he can transform you from the inside out causing your life to be prosperous while bringing Him all the honor and glory. Never to succumb to the negative emotions, thoughts and beliefs that causes you to remove yourself from the people that God has chosen to carry you. Now think about a person that you can connect with because if we need a good support system ourselves we first must become a good support system for someone else.

Looking to the Lord as your source for everything and not to other people, as He is your spiritual GPS, divinely guiding you to these connections displays a greater level of spiritual maturity and trust as His child. Avoid the need to isolate yourself from those that support and love you by maintaining a daily prayer life because the adversary has devised plots, ploys and schemes to keep your mind in ruins. John 10:10 says, *"the enemy came to steal, kill and destroy."* Embrace the people that will hold you accountable for your actions as this helps you to remain grounded in your thinking and it ultimately leads all of us to having a sound mind. A time will come in your life where you have to disconnect from those that you have called friends as your consciousness ascends to a higher level of thinking, causing you to re-evaluate the individuals who engage with you in low vibrational conversations, that keep you down in the dump after talking to them, and approve or justify your excuses for why your life is not working. Remember the things that you will not take responsibility for will keep you unmotivated when there is a need for a positive shift to take place in your thinking. So, if you are ignorant to what is already yours, it can be taken. God came that we may have life and have it more abundantly but the conditions of your mind have to be healed first then your life of abundance will pursue you instead of you pursuing it. Everything that you need to succeed in life, to walk in your divine power and in the fullness of what it is you desire is inside of you. Now your life has the potential to escalate to a prosperous place, bringing you to a place of serenity and contentment. As the thoughts of man controls, and guides his life, and destiny, maintaining your relationships by staying plugged in with the people that genuinely support you, and reject the thoughts that no longer serve your greatest good will cause you not to live in a sewer. Sinking into the quick sand of carnal and fleshy desires is exactly what the enemy is counting on you to do. How does he do this? By planting disempowering thoughts and suggestions in your mind, as your thoughts are the building blocks to your belief system. You will be held accountable for every thought that you allow to stay stuck in your head. Stay connected to your inner circle. The scripture tells us to submit to the Lord, resist the devil and he will flee from you.

The key to defeating carnal thinking happens when a person keeps their mind washed with the word of God. Every time the enemy brings a thought into your mind that opposes that of what you know to be the truth, you have to delete it from the space of your mind at that moment. You can't think on it because you're giving it permission to create unhealthy patterns of thought in your soul. As you gain the knowledge of how to use kingdom principles things will fall in place easily and effortlessly. Having a lack of knowledge means you're operating in the spirit of ignorance giving the enemy full access to you. There will be plenty of opportunities for you to be led by your emotions, feelings----the flesh. The easiest thing to do is to do whatever the flesh wants you to do. That means being nasty, unfriendly, argumentative, rude, snobbish, religious, and etc. If we're going to conquer our flesh we're going to have to discipline ourselves (practice) and not act on our own negative emotions. When you walk in the flesh know that it will affect your present, your future and any potential meaningful relationship you might have. All of God's beautiful creation should be showing forth improvement in the transformation of the soul and their spirit man, in which, we define spiritual maturity as a *"believer."* The issues that have been a dilemma in your life six months ago should not be evident in your present reality. It's time to grow, flourish, thrive, expand and improve. It is time for the body of Christ to grow up if what you are desiring is to grow higher in the things of the Lord. Elevating your thinking comes first. There won't be a promotion until you do. Knowing the right thing to do and not doing it isn't going to cut it either folks. Obedience is not just a choice we passively make it's a commandment. Therefore, it doesn't matter if you don't feel like being christlike in an ungodly situation or not. What is important is making a choice to always do the right thing. This is called *"Character"* and *"Integrity Building"* so allow the Holy Spirit to do whatever he needs to do within you. The unhealthy cycles and limiting belief's that we go through and continually struggle with are those things we need to improve and work on. You can't stay stuck on the steps and advance to new realms and dimensions in God. There will be times that God will choose not to change our problems. Instead, He will decide to transform us from within and teach us that His grace is sufficient. Sometimes, we put too much emphasis on the external and not enough on the internal. The internal part of man is what needs to be healed first then healing will spread to the outside. Work at bringing wholeness from within so what you desire can show up in the external facets of your life. Have you ever asked God too change something in your life? And he responded with a big fat NO! My grace is sufficient for you. It's not my intention to change your circumstances I'm going to change you. During dark times like these it teaches you and I how to become totally dependent and reliant on God. In order for your situation to change the conditions of your heart have to be healed. There were times in my own life that I asked God to deliver me from chronic pain and He didn't. In those moments God taught me not to war against His will just cooperate with what He was doing in my life. My perception about pain and struggle received a huge makeover. Rom. 8:28 says, *"All things work together for the good of them who love the Lord; That are called according to his purposes."* Yes, the purposes that God has for our life not our own purposes. Constantly, I pleaded with God to deliver me from suffering with this pain but he spoke to my spirit during a season of darkness in my soul and said, *"In your weakness I will make you strong. Apart from me you can do nothing but with me you can do all things."* This was not what I wanted to hear so because of that God had to do a great work within me. Boy! I struggled with this terribly. Aren't you glad God is patient, understanding and longsuffering? After all, if we don't suffer as Christ did, we can't reign with Him in The Kingdom of Heaven. The true son's and daughter's that are chosen and not just called comes to a position and posture of authentic submission after going through Jonah's ministry. Now if you have fasted, tried to bargain a deal with God, prayed and done everything that you know how to do and your situation still has not changed. It is the Lord telling you He's out to change you and not your circumstances. Give up on trying to manipulate God because He's not going to alter the assignment you've been given. No matter how special or close you think you are to Him. Why? So you can know how to operate in the anointing and still be effective in the midst of your adversity and suffering. You will lead others with love, and compassion, without judgement, because you will look at yourself as the Rahab, the Peter or the Paul that comes to you for prayer and help. Yes, it's a struggle but it is for your own good. Stop trying to figure God out because you can't. The only thing you will end up doing is frustrating yourself instead of walking in the divine will that God has already predestined for your life. Maintain a good connection with your support system. I'm referring to that inner circle. Those faithful few people that has always been there for you while everybody else dropped out of your life like how rotten fruit falls off of a tree. Our job is to have faith in God and speak those things that be not as though they were here now. Not waiting until you can visibly see with the natural eye to believe God. That is not faith. Heb. 11:1 says, *"Now faith is the substance of things hoped for and the evidence of things not seen."* With the heart we believe not with our mind. Secondly, having a teachable spirit brings illumination to your spirit man which is needed because you ultimately play a role in your own deliverance. You want to be free? Put your hand on the door knob, turn it and walk out. The choice is yours not God's. Pray and ask God to help you bring your fleshly thinking under subjection by the word, so you can develop healthy habits to live a healthy life. This is something you absolutely can't do on your own. It is going to require you to use the knowledge and skill you have acquired over time, through life's lessons and experiencies. We really need the Lord so don't fool yourself into thinking that you can handle the *"flesh"* on your own. But if you so happen to debate this truth, failure will always be your verdict.

The Lord is waiting and willing to help. Ask Him no matter how many times you have to inquire of God's assistance. God doesn't get impatient with you like some people would. He's not exhausted with your continual inquiries for help or neediness for Him. Dependency is what God is desiring from humanity. This is attractive to God because He appreciates the fact a person has come to the end of themselves and realized on their own they can't do anything without Him. It's hard to *"kick against the prick."* The apostle Paul tells us all about it in the new testament. The Heavenly Father will never put more on you than you can bare. (Jas. 1:2), *"My brethren, count it all joy when ye fall into divers temptations."* When your negative emotions rises up against you to provoke what you know to be the truth cast them down. Don't allow those demonic anchors to be planted, take root and produce fruit in your heart. Don't water it. Whatever you feed it will grow and if you starve something it will die. Therefore, when you start allowing your negative emotions and belief's to dictate your life you will begin to make poor choices and decisions. God is monitoring how we are responding to trouble. Change your thermostat! If you are murmuring and complaining about how bad a situation is stop it! Your words have life in them. Everytime you do this you're taking a step backward and not forward. Creating more negative people and circumstances to turn your world upside down. So when things like this show up, don't ask how in the world could this happen. Don't even attempt to change other people because you are not God. (Matt. 7:3) focus on the *"beam"* that's in your own eye because the true enemy is the enemy *"inner me"* within us. We are real good at pointing the finger at other people because we don't want to confront and be responsible for our own faults. It's easier to blame someone else and make them feel horrible about confronting and dealing with their personal demon's because it takes all the responsibility off of us. Wrong! It's shows you up big time and it's going to haunt you until you take action and change your life.

Dedicate the remainder of your existence to getting yourself healthy, mind, spirit and body. And always continue doing well for others-------don't get tired and weary in doing good because you will reap a good harvest if you refuse not to give up. Be encouraged in knowing that God is a rewarder of those who diligently seek him. Gal. 6:9, *"The Lord will always compensate you for what you have lost or for what you didn't get just like he did for Hannah."* Obedience to God is a key to one of The Kingdom's Principles on receiving a worthy portion. Getting concerned and staying concerned about the things of the Lord are beneficial to your life and spiritual growth as a believer. That means your time, your witness, service, finances and your entire being. Although life is challenging and at times unpredictable, thank God in all things. He is faithfully walking with you to get you to your expected end. He will take every avenue he possibly can to get the provision and blessing to you, through you and in your life. Through a devoted prayer life with meditation, communion, fasting, application and reading the word of God daily you will receive revelation that will guide you to reaching your souls mission in this life. You will know the true character of God as you align yourself with Him, then gain the know how to go about doing things His way. To get answers to the prayers that you thought were impossible, to gain total victory over your flesh, to bring stability in your soul so you can have a healthy mind, then ultimately experience a healthy life. Personally, I have learned how to effectively hear the voice of God, obey the spirit and silence the carnal mind. Anything or anyone that you withdraw your attention from has no more power over you to influence you in any way. A major part of my profound spiritual growth and development in the Lord was birthed through my pain and suffering on all levels, and when I positioned myself to receive his way of life and not my own. My idea of how to do life was not working so I found myself at a fork in the road. Realizing I was going to humble myself, become vulnerable and let my father put all of my broken pieces back together again. You know those intimate pieces that we're afraid to tell people because we have a fear of being judged? I didn't care what people thought about me anymore because their opinion's about me didn't matter after all. It was what I thought about myself that was sabotaging everything that God was trying to give me. So, I let out a shofar cry, threw my hands up and screamed help from my belly. If you stay with God and delight yourself in him he will give you the desires of your heart. Sincere prayer will position you for pure worship and replace your desires with the desires of the father. He will give you a heart to live for him and feed his sheep. (Gal.5:17) *"For the flesh lusteth after the flesh, and the spirit against the flesh: and these are contrary one to another: So that you can't do the things that you would."* With a continued walk with God while keeping yourself sensitive to His spirit, you'll become successful in bringing your flesh under subjection where it belongs. Because now you have the understanding that you are no longer your own but have been bought with a price. A temple of God endowed with power, filled with precious ointment, and precious treasures.

CHAPTER FOUR

"THE PROCESS OF IN BETWEEN"

Learning how to activate your inner higher state of being by literally tapping into the reality of who you are as a *"Spirit"* gives grace permission to be a pillar of cloud by day and a pillar of fire by night for you while in this dark season of the mind. Causing epiphany after epiphany to illuminate your insight and perception through the realization that you are more than your physical body. Have you found yourself in a night season saying *"Lord, if I could just get a hint or a clue from you right now I'll be alright."* Or better yet, I can navigate through this maze of a cornfield a little bit easier if you would just radiate a ray of light on the path that I'm on. Why did you choose this difficult path for me anyway? Surely, there's a path that I can take that has the least resistance. I'm really freaking out right about now. This is taking too long, and I'm going in circles oblivious in the darkness. I've hit a fork in the road and I don't know what direction I need to take to get to the other side of this dilemma. God, did you forget that I'm out here in the middle of no where trying to get to the *"place?"* The place that you promised me. This is a journey I must walk alone and I've come to far to turn around and go back but a part of me wants to turn around as the unfamiliar causes fear, worry, anxiety and doubt. If God loves me, why would He place me in this situation? Why would he show me the promise then place me in the middle of nowhere? An unfruitful, dry and painful place.

Everybody that I thought was with me has turned their back on me saying *"Surely God wouldn't allow you to go through all of this."* Especially not for this long. God have mercy on me and guide me out of this maze. Have you been given a big dream, vision or promise? Only to find yourself in the bottom of a pit? Or a foreigner in a strange land? If that's not bad enough, God is now giving you the silent treatment. What a painful place for anyone to be in but it's purposeful. Why isn't He talking to me? I was certain my connection to heaven was on point. He's the master teacher and when a teacher is giving a student a test there is no dialogue going on in the classroom. The teacher wants to see how much you have learned and how you will either react or respond to all the pressures and problems of life. Yes, this is the process that we all have to go through in order to get to the other side of the promise. Yeah, the *"In Between Place"* that God didn't bother to give us details about. The place that looks nothing like your promised land. God didn't ask us what route would be better suitable for us to take in getting to the promised land because He doesn't have to . The way has been predetermined by God for reasons that are of no concern of ours. If He wanted to take you a different route other than what you thought, He should have, He could have. In case you forgot He is the creator of *"All"*, there is no-one that can counsel Him or oppose His will.

Right now, life is putting your faith on trial to see if you have what it takes or not to get to the other side of this stubborn problem. Will you endure this hardness like the soldier God created you to be? Or will you give up by tapping out? Will you have a miscarriage and abort the promise? Or will you carry the dream to full term?

There is no time for indecisiveness. You don't have time to debate with doubt while you're fighting and trying to keep your head above the water. Standing firm in your faith is simply evicting the enemy from renting space in your mind. You have the power to accept or reject what thoughts become planted in your mind, realizing that you can't run away from things that scare you, make you feel uncomfortable, intimidate and cause you to be afraid. It's only a process that means there is a beginning and there is an ending. The closer you get to birthing your promise the more God stretches you because He has to make sure you can accomodate what He placed in your womb to carry.

41

"*Belief*" is the main component a person has to have if you're going to do anything significant in your life. You must make a decision right now to enter into a marriage covenant with faith, trust and divorce doubt with no hopes of a reconciliation. It's going to take your own belief and not anyone else's. Every person has to carry their own cross regardless of how good of a relationship you have with someone else. Learn to have and understand the importance of developing a great relationship with self which is derived from the relationship you have with God. If you can't get along with yourself you will not succeed in keeping peace and harmony in any of your relationships. You'll know what kind of a relationship you have with God by the relationships you have with the people in your life. If you don't have authentic and unwavering faith, Pharaoh and his army will drown you in the Red Sea for sure. God's intention was for the Red Sea to consume and destroy your enemies not you. Granting you access to total freedom and victory to serve Him without any reservations nor limitations, as there are no more open, bleeding wounds and holes in your soul.

Romans 8:16-17, "*The Spirit itself beareth witness with our Spirit, that we are the children of God. And if children of, then heirs of God, and joint heirs with Christ.*" Renounce everything and everyone in your life that does not bring forth God's divine nature. This is so profound, and one of the greatest, sincere prayers you will ever pray to the father, which is my personal opinion and how I myself found it to be true in my life. In between you getting to that place you desire this type of "*true prayer*" is born. Right from an intimate relationship that has been developed through your personal time with God causing you to conceive and become pregnant with destiny. Also be mindful of this while you are in the wilderness holding the vision God gave you hostage as you navigate your way out of the darkness and chaos. Because when you're in a real battle all you have is the promise that God gave you to keep you going. There is no pushing and pulling against God. You either sink or swim, live or die. This is the prayer language heaven is listening for. God is evaluating how you respond to trouble. Ask yourself what can I do for you father? Instead of asking God to do you a favor. Prayer doesn't mean giving God a wish list of everything we need and want him to do for us. When a person can seek to understand what the will of God is for their life, without asking him to perform any miracles, this is a sign of true humility, spiritual maturity and authentic servitude. Ask the Lord to reveal to you who you are? You must know your identity. Why you were created? What your Purpose is? And what role do you play in the Kingdom of God? What is your Assignment on earth?

It is the will of God that we are always aware of how we are living at all times on a day to day basis. There are people who have you under a microscopic lens to see if your life is in alignment with the word of God. Even more importantly, you are wearing the precious name of the Lord which is His reputation so don't dishonor it. We have not been created to go through life just hanging in there, hardly getting by, always in lack, depressed, and hoping and wishing we were blessed. You are blessed (happy, envied, favored, empowered) because He said you were but you must receive this truth in your mind and heart because your spirit already bears witness of the truth. You have to keep a positive perception (self-image) of the Father because how you literally view God is going to show up in your life. So if you grew up without a natural father in your home, this will translate to your relationship with your Heavenly Father as well as with others. There will be waves of fear, codependency issues, a lack of trust and honor surfacing in your life while you're fighting your way out of the in between place, because there is no room for these vampire energies in your future.

Dig deep into the word of God as a farmer would do before planting seed in the earth, then apply the principles of the kingdom that you're now mastering. Unlock those self-made prison doors and pull down the walls of Jericho that are fixated in your mind. There will be no visible sign of liberty in your life without revelation and self-awareness that you are the master of your thoughts. The enemy fights you by the lack of knowledge that you don't know about God. He tries to poke holes in the truth and cause you to question what God is teaching you but you must stay in the mode of hearing.

Romans 10:17, *"Faith comes by hearing and hearing by the word of God."* Notice hearing is mentioned twice in this scripture. Some things we are going to have to learn by repetition----------------that means doing it over and over again until it becomes a habit then a positive behavior. Once again this is why you are in that in between place of struggle and your destiny. In applying this kingdom principle, you will begin to discover who you are and when you do proclaim it everyday in Jesus name. This is what it means to operate and access heaven by using the keys of David. Hearing the word of God one time is not going to stimulate your faith nor your belief system. You are going to have to hold yourself accountable in getting into a good bible believing church where the true, unadulterated word of God is being teached, preached and demonstrated. Then, the Holy Spirit will quicken your spirit to receive the truths and sayings of Jesus which is going to cause dominant change in all aspects of your life. Not the sayings you have been exposed too in your childhood, and etc.

As children we didn't learn our ABC's the first time we heard them. It is vital in our Christian life that we know these things so we will know how to apply them in a practical way, and in our day to day lives so we'll become synchronized with the plan that God has for our life. Begin speaking words of faith not unbelief. Out of the abundance of the heart the mouth speaks. Remember that saying *"what you don't know won't hurt you"* that's a lie straight from the enemy. Satan the father of lies. What you don't know can literally destroy you and cause you to live outside of the will of God. You will have a measure of success but never reach your full potential. That's why some of our lives are being destroyed because we choose to believe the traditional sayings and teachings that we have been pre-exposed to by religion, society, social circles, the educational system, culture, family members, and etc. My saying of empowerment is *"If you don't know you can't change it and if you refuse knowledge you will never know how."*

When the Spirit of Truth comes you will breakthrough to a life of success, contentment, joy and peace. This is the will of the Father. If we keep our mind focused on the Lord and meditate on the word daily, we won't engage in the enemies deceptions. Now you need to create the image in your mind of what you want your life to look life by mentally rehearsing it over and over again. It's significant in our transformation. God knows that change *"hurts"* and it's very uncomfortable. He also knows growth and expansion can't come if a person stays in their comfort zone. God will never force His will nor His plan for your life on you. You have to be able to receive it in all humility and in faith. The Father is a perfect gentlemen. God loves to be celebrated and not tolerated so you have to create an atmosphere that will be conducive for him. Genesis 8-10 encourages us not to try and hide our sins from God because when we do we break fellowship with Him. Sin divides us from God and obedience keeps us in His presence. This is where God wants you so He can instruct you, tell you what you need to get done and how to get it done. God is omniscience (all knowing) we can't fool Him. It behooves us to get real with ourselves. Face it head on and you won't walk in the Spirit of Torment. This is the divine will of God------doing things His way so that you get the desired results you are believing for. Our will (ego) has to die so His will for our lives can come forth. God will always take the weak things of this world to confound the wise. Let your life reflect love, the glory of God, patience, temperance and restraint. Gods will is that we let the power of the Holy Spirit lead us and keep our vision alive so our true purpose in life can be revealed. All of our giftings, abilities, knowledge and talents were given to us only to be used for the greatest good of all mankind, for the Kingdom of God which brings Him glory. Whatever the Father has entrusted you with, give Him the glory and never give self a medal of honor. Don't allow pride and the spirit of self-centeredness to cloud your thinking. It is not because of your own ability. Therefore, never boast and brag on self. Only on the creator and not the gift. Always worship the giver and not the gifts and talents you possess.

The majority of us are trying to obtain success by the standards of this world while neglecting the importance of finding what God has desired for you His way. As you use His schematic plan, you'll be following the right instructions that's going to lead you to the right destination. What has the Lord impressed in your heart to do? What has He revealed to you through vision and dreams? What has that man or woman of God spoken in your life? This is what God wants you too pursue. I adjure you by the power and the authority of Jesus Christ to go forth in boldness to be that world changer. Your task is essential in bringing God's plan to fruition so get busy. Exodus 3 tells us that we need to have confidence in who Christ says we are instead of how we feel about ourselves. Do you know who you are? Or are you seeking your identity from others and through the things of this world?

God is a very strategic Father so with an intimate relationship with Him, you will develop a right concept of thinking. It's not what other people think of you that stops your progress. Yes, you guessed it correctly it is the internal dialogue you're having with yourself. Another key factor is the importance of you finding out who God truly is so you can imitate Him. If you never take the time to know God you will never find out who you really are. It doesn't matter who told you who you are. There will still be some dissatisfaction lingering around down on the inside of you, until you can believe it for yourself, then you will ultimately become it.

God is a deliberate creator who decided without any argument or counsel from anything that He created, nor did it require an explanation from anyone, that He chose to house His spirit within our physical bodies which makes us one with the Father. We have been given His innate ability for a reason. I'll give you a little hint go and create like He did. Move the mountains of impossiblities in your life by exercising what you believe. Whatever you do don't ask people if they think you can do it or not. God already told you you could so do it. Our problems aren't confessing the faith scriptures. It's the lack of application that hinders evidence of us manifesting what we have been speaking and declaring. We have to believe what we are confessing. To every promise of God their is a "*key*", a Kingdom Principle that you must learn before receiving. You have to learn how to stimulate your belief system by doing something that corresponds to what you believe. This gives you access to the promises of God. Put your faith into action. Faith without works is "*dead*" non-profitable. We are going to have to work our faith. Start putting things into motion by what you say and what you do. That's what energy is and it can't ever be destroyed. Go pick out your dream home, declare your healing while your body is in pain, pick out your car, the wedding dress, declare your debts are supernaturally canceled. It shouldn't matter how silly it seems to you or how strange you appear to other people just do it and watch God comply with your faith. It's a Universal Law and God can't turn His back on His word. His laws have been recorded and legislated in the courtroom of heaven, as His voice echoes, and vibrates in the sphere of time and through every galaxy.

God always looks over His word to perfect, perform and execute it. He's listening to hear who is speaking the word so He can manifest Himself. He created us to speak what we wanted to see come to pass in our life. We frame our world by the words we speak into the atmosphere. When darkness hindered the light from coming forth, God spoke and said "*let there be light*" and light came forth. He didn't have a conversation with the angels to ask them "*Do you think I can do it?*" No, He said what He wanted to see and the rest is history. This same power and authority is within you so speak to that sickness, lack, marriage, business, circumstance or problem that is hindering you from walking in the place that God wants for you. We have to believe the word of God and live uprightly before Him in order for the word to work for us. The word of God will work for you but you have to work it. Give up those talks of failure and defeat, stop murmuring and complaining about your problem. Start engaging in positive conversations so good things can show up for you and the people you love, and watch provision and blessings come forth in every facet of your life. Why? Because your belief system has changed and it's giving you the results you really want...........All aspects of you are divinely aligned to the source in which all things exist. The seen and the unseen. What is seen in the physical realm is an illusion and what is unseen is real. As it is in the natural so shall it be in the spirit.

God never told us to talk about our problem. He instructed us to speak to it. What are you doing? Are you murmuring about how long it's taking? And complaining about how bad the situation is? It's not going to hurry the process along. The more you complain the longer you will remain in that condition. No matter what we say we will eat the fruit of our spoken words as they are life. Creating what was vibrated because death and life are in the power of your tongue so guard your mouth.

The Book of Proverbs tells us that we are snared by the words that come out of our mouth. The words that you speak in your present reality will show up in your future. No matter what we sow we will reap it so make sure it's the harvest you are wanting. Start replacing negative thoughts with a positive image and negative confessions with a positive word. We have to let the enemy know that we are not afraid to exercise the power and authority that God has given us. Let the enemy know you have confidence in the word by declaring it from your lips. If you were a drug addict that was serious about sobriety you would replace that wrong behavior with good behavior and develop positive friendships, right? There is no way that you will maintain an ounce of freedom if you keep the same friends and continue going to the same unhealthy places that you use to. Vision yourself healed, delivered, happy, and successful before you have evidence of it in the natural. How does it feel? Philippians 2:5-8 says, *"let this mind be in you as it was in Christ Jesus."* Too many of us tolerate certain situations and circumstances in our life because you think you have to. If you want to experience continual victory in your life there is no room for laziness. God will never promote the person who slacks only those who are diligent. Some people just sit back and say well I'm just going to wait on God. In all actuality, God is waiting on you to put your faith in Him with works. Faith without works is dead. Work your faith-------do something...Even if you are afraid...Take a step.

II Timothy tells us to study to show ourselves approved a workmen need not be ashamed rightly dividing the word of truth. When we study the word of God he reveals himself to us in ways we couldn't perceive that he could. He gives us creative ideas, solutions to problems, direction, wisdom, discernment, knowledge, and understanding when we pursue him. Revelation feeds our spirits and starves all of our doubts to death. A double minded man is unstable in all his ways not just some but ALL! There is something about that faithful and persistent person the bible says this person will abound in blessings. Why remain in a place that no longer serves you?....Press! Press! Press!

James 4:7 says, *"Submit to God resist the devil and he will flee from you."* When the enemy tries to give you something you just don't take it. Don't accept anything from him because the cost will be greater than what you will be willing to pay for it. Sin will always make you stay longer in a mess, and it will take you further than you ever wanted to go, and it will make you pay a price you never intended to pay. Remember the enemy breaks his covenant. He'll give you a boat without a life jacket knowing that you couldn't swim and then expect you to get back to the shore the best way you can. Then he will bring accusations against you, condemn you and make you feel terrible about taking him up on his offer. Now you're all depressed, oppressed, irritable, unstable and questioning your salvation and the call that God has on your life. When the mental pain is excruciating you have to have faith and hold on to the promises of God. These will be the times for you to place your vision in front of you. No matter what it looks like just believe God and wait for your appointed time. As uncomfortable as it may sound and as weird as you're going to feel, talking to yourself is what you're going to have to do to survive this drought. Now stand still and become stable in your emotion's regardless of what is going wrong in your life, so you can see the salvation of the Lord. You're not going to have a nervous breakdown and die! Although you may feel like you are, you will get through this madness. These are birthing pains. I know you want to push but don't. Just breathe in and out. Chaos only came to shift you in the right direction. While you are swimming in the red sea of problems and climbing mountains of impossibilities continue doing good for others and pray for those who say all manner of evil against you falsely. Greater is he that is in you than he that is in the world. Having the reassurance that the Lord will never leave us nor forsake us......This is the way God has chosen for you to get to "The Divine Will of God." Yes, I know it's not the way you think you should be going right? I said the same thing. God could have taken an easier route right? Yes, but His ways and thoughts are not like ours. He knows the perfect way that you should take. When God gets through with you you will be an awesome child of God. Oh how you will shine bright as a diamond after you've survived the process of the fire. Let Him finish what He has started in you. He is all powerful to do it so go through the process and give birth to your dream..Now push.

The wings of despair should drive you closer to God instead of moving yourself farther away from Him. If you remove yourself from the presence of God you will begin to see things drop off, rot, decay and die in your life. During your time of pursuing the will that God has for your life be aware of how you relate to other people. Sow finances, love, encouragement, compassion, prayer, fasting and give of yourself wholeheartedly, completely and totally to the things of God. Daily read and study the word of God to ensure that you will have the proper knowledge and skill to help you start dissecting your life to bring about positive change with lasting results. Everything and everyone that is sucking the life out of you diligently trying to keep you in bondage and captivity get rid of them. This is the true defintion of what and enemy is. Your destiny is calling and it has to be your main focus. Visualize it everyday until you start finding yourself dreaming about it and then begin doing something daily that pertains to it. Every impoverished thing that has happened in your life God is going to turn it around for your good and give you a powerful testimony. We overcome by the blood of the lamb and by the word of our testimony. That means obstacles have to come so we can have something to fight for and overcome. It's like a person who has a fear of spiders or heights but without fear how can one develop courage? How can one pursue abundance without the experience of lack? Begin to acknowledge the Lord in all your ways so He can direct your steps, and wherever He leads you that's where you need to go, and only do what He has told you to do....No more..When you get there if you're not received shake the dust off of your feet and leave a testimony in that place.. Your job is to obey His voice and not to worry if you are received or believed because they are rejecting the spirit of the Lord and not you. It's about His will and not our own.

Anytime you take a step in the direction of your purpose in life, there will be great resistance from the enemy because he can't stand the fact that you now see yourself as God does, and you're no longer satisfied with your present situation. You are ready for change. If you are hungry and thirsty the Lord will make it a priority to fill you. Don't stop in the middle of getting to where you desire to be strenghten yourself and continue moving forward. Some people are content in life but don't ever become satsified with where you are because God has much, much more for you to experience.

LOVE ONE ANOTHER

John 15:17, *"These things I command you, that you love one another."* Loving others is a main ingredient to having authentic and long lasting success. Did you know that true success is the journey that we travel while looking to encounter our life purpose? It's all the series of events the good and the not so good events that we go through. All the up's and down's, the high's and the low's and the in and out's. Helping us to comprehend that how we relate to others should be important to us, because it's a reflection of who you really are anyway. Would you hurt or injure your own body? Not if you love yourself you wouldn't. I don't know why we try to reach out before we reach within ourselves because we just simply can't give away what we simply don't have. Oh, I know why people do that it's because of what we've been taught in this *"world"* or *"babylonian system."* Our minds have been conditioned to think wrong, with lack and limitation because you've conformed your manner of thinking to the systems of this world, instead of mastering your thoughts through the word of God. *"For God so loved the world that he gave his only begotten son,"* John 3:16. Whenever we can love like Christ has loved us then and only then will people know that we are truly God's disciples. How can we say we love God whom we have NEVER seen and we see our brothers and sisters daily and have hate, malice, jealousy and enviousness in our hearts? How hypocritical is that. You say and do not. That's another reason why some of our lives are depleted and our prayers have been hindered. When you stand praying before a righteous and a Holy God stand in a posture of forgiveness so you can be forgiven. Change your mind as you allow the truth of God's word to renew your heart right now and do the right thing by all people, Amen.

There is no way that God is going to over look us and bypass the way we make others feel. No way! God is a holy and a righteous God that renders vengeance, justice and mercy at His own will. There is no darkness nor variableness in Him and it shouldn't be in us either. Unless you are not of His fold. It is the Lord who touches the heart of men to bless you and present you with great opportunities. Jesus needed His disciples and we need each other. We are the body of Christ with many members and different functions. You will never get the things that you desire in your life nor will you ever get to the place that you long to be on your own. Nor with the favorite few you like and prefer over everybody else. We need each other. Rahab, the harlot played an important role in freeing the men of God. Which secured her in the genealogy of the "*messiah*" Jesus Christ. God just designed it that way so we can learn how to have better, fulfiling and committed friendships/relationships. God is able to do exceedingly, abundantly above all that we can ask or think according to the power that worketh on the inside of us (Ephes. 3:20). Never put limitations on God nor on your own ability as His child because you won't receive the fullness of what He wants to give you. Get God out of the box you have Him in, keep an open mind and watch great things unfold right before your eyes.

GETTING WISDOM AND UNDERSTANDING

Wisdom is not the person who knows alot. Wisdom is when you put what you know about God and life into practice (application) in everyday experiences and not by how many degrees you have acquired. Now go ahead and start applying what you have learned to the circumstances, and issues that surround you. When we walk with God we're being wise and when we walk in foolishness by leaning to our own understanding we're walking on our own. If you need wisdom ask God and He will be glad to give it you. It's free. How wise is it that we trust the banks with our money, we trust the doctors to treat us and we can't give our trust to the Lord? The creator of everything. Prov. 3:1-8 was written so that we would take heed to our ways, gain knowledge and wisdom so that we could be directed, and learn how to operate in the Spirit of Discernment. It's not enough for us to have head knowledge and be oblivious to the things of God. God wants us to be wise, having the ability to use what we know and make good judgements.

God wants us to have stability in our lives. Some people are lacking the ability to be stable and firm. Instead they are living fragmented lives never accomplishing what it is that they really desire because they lack focus and the importance of being committed, and sticking with a goal until the end. Your dream is not going to fall out of the sky and into your hand. Mal. 3:6 says, *"I am the Lord and I change not."* He is the same yesterday, today and forever. God requires the same thing of us. He wants us to be people that are consistent and not be spiritually bipolar because He has to know that He can count on us when the winds of life threatens our promise. Learning to do what is just, love mercy and walk humbly before Him. This is the will of God that we learn to do all that has been written in the word. *"Thou shalt love the Lord thy God with all thy heart, and with all thy soul, and with all thy mind. This is the first and greatest commandment."* You're going to have to believe in your heart that He is God and of course you know you have to obey Him, and live exactly like He tells you to-----striving for this everyday of your life. *"Straight is the gate, and narrow is the way, which leadeth unto life, and few there that find it,"* Matt. 7:14. Start seeking the Lord more than you ever have. I believe in my heart that God is going to do things quickly. Your friends and family aren't going to understand how you have progressed so fast. Tell them you have been in the presence of the Lord. Your set time of acceleration is here! Now you have to have a willingness to do the Fathers will and have confidence in Him to work in you, and through you for His good pleasure. Be forgiving and always repent (inward change) when you have done something contrary to the word of God. Or if a person says you have offended them apologize immediately and mean it in your heart. Your heart is the second compartment of your soul. It's the seat of your emotion's and where all the issues of life flow through. Don't justify your behavior deal with it. Be mindful that you are pursuing the will God has for you. Let this be your main focus and vision yourself at the destination spot! There will be road blocks, yield signs, and hurdles so jump over them, go around them, or go under them. If God be for you there is no devil in hades that can be against you. Remember the battle belongs to God and victory belongs to you. God is telling us that when He allowed us to be born again the *"New Birth"* does not have it's source in the human will but the Divine Will of God. When you are really born again you don't look to other people nor anything around you to meet your needs. That means your mother and father are not your source, your job, friends, or your bank account. Your source for everything is the Lord Jesus Christ. Although, God allows us to have places of employment your pay check is not your resource! It's not what takes care of you nor is it your source of making sure that all of your needs are met. Your paycheck you receive is your seed. Yes, that's right it is your seed for you to sow to make sure you are never in lack or want. When you're in the will of God for your life there will be no argument in your flesh. When He wakes you up in the middle of the night to pray you get up without argument. You just lay the plate down and don't eat if you're called to fast. You will throw your hands up and say yes Lord I surrender all and I position myself so that you can do with me as you see fit. God is such a gentlemen so don't concern yourself with what's going to happen if you surrender all to Him. Once you do this you will be able to say God is my leader, my provider, my protector and friend. He means everything to me and I'm entrusting everything I have in His hands. I must warn you though that when you ask God to let His will be done in your life you better know what you are saying. If you have invited the Lord in that's all He wanted because He needs a vessel to work His will through. Now you need to give up the place that you are in right now regardless of how uncomfortable it is so that you can go to the next level in God. This can literally mean some of those people that started out with you may not finish with you because they are not connected to your destiny. God sees these people as venomous serpents, viper's, wolves in sheeps clothing and He will not allow someone to pollute and poision what He has invested so much in. You are an earthen vessel with hidden riches deposited down on the inside of you. I can honestly tell you there will be dark moments in your life. You will feel abandoned, isolated, rejected, forgotten, broken, crushed, forsaken, having a desire to give up, not called to do the task and complete emptiness. These were some of my personal feelings while I was in the wilderness trying to find my way to the promised land. The battle in my mind intensified but I perservered, cried and prayed out to God fervently because my burning desire was to fulfil the plan of God in my life and I was determined in doing so. You can do it! Stay consistent and remain diligent because it will bring you into your Canaan (The Land of Promise). Always keep your vision in front of you and never ever allow the enemy to deter you and get you off course with distractions. This is His desire that you will not reach your destiny and fulfill your dreams. The devil is a liar! Go forth in the name of Jesus because greater is He that is within you than he that is in the world. Concentrate, focus, and meditate on everything that is honest, just, lovely, of a good report so you can walk in the favor of God and birth your dream and destiny. (Phil. 4:8) Don't pay attention to your family and friends who are acting crazy around you because you have decided to go after your vision. Come out from amongst them and be seperated to be used for the masters good will. Remember it's not how you start but it's how you finish. The race is not given to the swift but to the one that will endure to the end. Embrace this spiritual journey while embarking on the divine will of God for your life.

CHAPTER FIVE

"CREATING WITH INTENTION"

＋◆＋◆＋◆＋

Are you being intentional in your prayer life? Asking exactly what you want and not what you think is acceptable according to your own standards or beliefs. Or maybe you're praying from a place of lack and neediness based on the opinions of what other people think you should have and be grateful for. Are you living a life on purpose? And not haphazardly? Did you know that it was God's desire and intention for earth to operate just like heaven, with order and without chaos before the fall of Adam and Eve? God thought and imagined how He wanted everything to be before He spoke it into existence. He was intentional in His creation not once considering the possibilities of what could go wrong. After God focused on what He wanted He began creating those things by speaking it into physical form. What are you speaking into your life? As He told Adam *"you name the animals and whatever you call them that's what it is."* Can you feel the power in the authority that you and I have? Co-creators of our own reality and life exercising our kingdom authority. What are you thinking about during the day? And what are you calling things in your life? Is it what brings you success and happiness? First, you must know what you do want because if you don't life will remain consistent in presenting you with circumstances that you don't want. Whatever you are affirming on a daily basis your belief system, thoughts and emotions has to resonate with it. Everything has to be aligned with your spirit in order for the physical manifestation of a persons desires takes shape and form in their now. A great place to start would be to practice thinking on the things that make you feel good, and by being grateful for what you have instead of focusing on everything you don't have right now. Are you producing whatever it is that you want? Are you expanding? What are you building to ensure your mark and legacy will exceed you when you're long gone? Are you being creative and innovative like God? Are you maximizing your gifts, talents and skills that God has given you to raise up more generals and disciples to impact your generation and community? This is such a high expectation from God to "*man*" his creation. Which no excuses will linger in his presence when you stand before him to give an account for the life you lived on earth. We all are accountable for every gift that we've been given so we must die empty and not full of greatness. One is to only create the life they want through the power of setting deliberate intentions when praying. This is the reason for your existence. Humanity is the highest expression of everything that God created because we were made in His likeness and His image. Did you know that if you're not happy with the life you have you can create the one you want by constantly thinking about what you do want? Imagine how you will feel in this new found life. Now focus on all the good you will do with these new opportuntites that you have now been given. This is how you produce what you want and bring forth the life you desire from the spiritual dimension to the earth realm where it will become tangible.

After God made man (Genesis 1:28), He blessed them and said be fruitful, multiply, and replenish the earth, and subdue it. Then man was given dominion by God. A believer is not to depend on the world to supply what they need as a child of God, because you have already been given everything you need by our creator. It is every students responsibility to develop their gifts and talents by gaining the knowledge that is needed for them to thrive in. We have to learn how to properly dominate, govern and rule in the environment God has placed us in. Everything that God created including the animals and other species have learned how to thrive in their own environment. The fish in the sea and the birds of the air, and etc. So what is our problem? Disbelief? Man does not believe in the infinite power of God within them to do the impossible by speaking things into existence. Why? Because they've allowed the voice of the enemy to cause them to distrust God and doubt what He said. How does this happen? It happens when a person only sees themselves as human and not a divine spirit. Although, it is God who touches the heart of men to bless us. We still are not to put our total trust and confidence in no one except the Lord. Our Heavenly Father is the great "I AM THAT I AM." The all sufficient one, our provision, and creator. God is a God of increase and multiplication and the same should reflect the life of the believer. Are you bearing fruit in your life? Are you positively affecting the lives of those who are in need? Is multiplication evident in your life today? If so praise God and if not lets work harder to produce good fruit. Jesus came to add and multiply our life so that it will be plentiful, productive, with demonstrations of the kingdom of God on earth. The enemy of our faith comes to subtract, divide, steal, kill and destroy. Having the lack of knowledge in what God says you have a right to have gives the enemy power over you in that area. How? Because you are in darkness to the truth. Everyone has the ability and power to create a better life. However, everyone won't develop their potential to do so due to a lack of diligence and desire. How does a person create one might ask? You have to use your own God given human imagination then focus on the end result regardless of the distractions the natural eye sees. Everything that has ever been created or will be created is first created in the imagination and mind of man. Whatever you want already exists. Are you constantly thinking about what you don't want and what you don't like? If so, this is exactly what you're going to get whether you like it or not. You placed an intention in the atmosphere by your thoughts (images) and it manifested. It just didn't give you what you probably really wanted right? God told Joshua to meditate on His word day and night. The head and heart has to enter into a covenant of belief in order to receive any of the promises of God. You must retrain your subconscious mind to think only what you want and set a postive emotion with it to bring it to pass. It is being done all the time but unrealized by so many people. This is called manifesting by default. But now you must learn how to use your imagination intentionally and deliberately. That means taking time for daily prayer and meditation in order to calm the mind, as this will bring balance to your thoughts that you are projecting from within. Now begin deliberately focusing only on what it is that you want and in time it will happen. As you begin clearing past belief blockages this will help you get to the place you want sooner rather than later. So that desire, dream, vision or business that God has purposed in your heart will show up when you least expect it to. Call it into existence through your words by faith in the name of Jesus Christ. Learn to live in the now. We successfully do this by using our God given human imagination to visualize ourself in the place we want to be in and by doing whatever it is we want to do before we actually get there. This is what the bible means by *"now faith is."* So call those things that be not as if they already were. Act just like you have whatever it is you've believed God for. Talk just like it to. We can only receive to the capacity we have in our Spirit, and what has been revealed to us by the Spirit of God. How in the world do I get the vision evident here on earth now? How do I get what I'm dreaming about in my mind into my bank account? You must first believe in the supernatural power of God and the ability you have been given as a co-creator. Then see it in the spiritual realm in order to have the true manifestation in the natural. As a man thinketh in his heart so is he. If you want your life to change then change the way you think and feel. Stop thinking on the things you don't want because it will manifest in your life. Decide on whatever it is you do want and only think on those thoughts and nothing else. Introduce your mind to a cycle of new images that are beneficial to the realilty you're desiring by mentally rehearsing them over and over again to master divine consciousness.

James 1:2 says, *"But be ye doers of the word and not hearers only deceiving your ownselves."* Too many believers are coming into the house of God having no valid evidence of fruit bearing in their lives. Have we forgotten about the great responsibility we have to God then to ourselves while we are present in this world? Stay mindful of these things when you have a desire to become complacent, unfrutiful, stagnant and sluggish. The Lord expects all of us as his children to be active participants in winning souls, with signs, miracles, and wonders following. And fund the kingdom to help the gospel be preached all over the world. There are so many hurting people who are waiting on us to speak a word of deliverance to their situation. How can we heal another person if we are bleeding and sick? We all have been called as God's ambassadors, and legislatures in this world to be a beacon of light to those who are walking in darkness and ignorance to the things of God. Become bold and let your light shine as you walk in the knowledge of the truth. God just might use you to be the one to change and impact your church, family, community and job for his glory. So let that bright light bring illumination so men can see your good works and glorify your father which is in heaven. Step out on faith! When the devil says you won't make it you need to open your mouth and boldly proclaim you are a liar! Stare him in the face and shout increase! increase! increase! in Jesus name. God said it believe it! If He spoke it, He will bring it to pass. You are His child and God is faithful to His word. This race is about the assignment that God has given you. You must fulfill your assignment and endure to the end. It is not for you to become boastful and lifted up in pride as your life increases with blessings. Neither material blessings nor a person's good merit will give them a sure place in heaven.

Always have a teachable and submissive spirit. God is a giving Father but be mindful that he does take away. This is the sovereignty of God. If you have any doubts about that read the book of Job, and He will testify it too. Secondly, never compete for position! This is a big No! No! and a huge setback to anyone going forth in the things that God has preordained for you. This is how you can disqualify yourself from being used by God after He indeed called you. For example if your name is not called before the congregation, or on a program you will not allow the spirit of offense from the enemy to get you bent out of shape, and hinder you from preaching the unadulterated gospel, and from walking in love. Underdeveloped and spiritually immature people will respond to life and circumstances in low states of consciousness because the voice of their ego is in charge of their thinking and decision making instead of the spirit man. When you know who you are in the kingdom there is no fighting or arguing for position. Promotion comes from God just in case you're looking to people for it. I Corinth. 3:7 says, "*So then neither is he that planteth anything neither he that watereth: but God that giveth the increase.*" No matter what seed we plant, how we may nurture it and cultivate it God is the only one that brings forth the harvest not us. This will erradicate the thoughts of those who want to receive the credit themselves--the glory belongs to God and remember He swore by His own holiness that He will never share His glory with anyone. That's right not one person. Give God the glory and not your know how or ability regardless of how effective and sufficient you think you are. God is the giver of every talent, gift and knowledge not your parents. This includes His most anointed earthen vessel. A person can't make anything happen for themselves apart from God. I don't care who you know and what hook-up you are trying to connect with. Your hook-up is in your prayer closet with the Father. Release whatever is in your hands and give it to God. Never let the enemy intimidate you into not sowing your seed in the kingdom. Give it to God in faith with expectation and provoke your dream to come to pass. Whatever realm you want to grow in you must first sow in that soil. To conclude, you must be faithful to that which pertaineth to another man before God will give you your own. God is evaluating our "*Stewardship*" and "*Obedience.*" Whatever you make happen for someone else that very thing will be reciprocated right back to you. It's The Universal Law Of Sowing And Reaping. Be fruitful and multiply and don't mishandle blessings, opportunities nor the people God entrusts to you.

When the opportunity comes for you to plant seed don't plant it in infertile ground, or in a place that Gods will is not being accomplished. Invest in people who invest in you. Be mindful of where you are sowing at all times. All soil is not good and furtile soil. Learn to recognize the anointing and partner with it. Always sow in a vision that is much greater than your own. And sow where you desire to be in life. While you are sowing I want you to position yourself in receiving the blessing because it is your birthright. Does a farmer plant seed and not expect to reap a harvest? Never compromise and violate the principles of God. Maintain your integrity, character, and be honest and just in all of your dealings. God has to prepare you and get you ready for what He's been longing to give you. If you're not responsible with the blessings you have been entrusted with, and if you don't have the right attitude in knowing what the purpose for your blessing is, God will not release it in your life because there is the potential of you losing it. Don't forfeit the promise. God will not give you something that you're not equipped for or mature enough to handle. Level up and grow up in the spiritual things of God. Spiritual maturation in every believer's life has to be mastered and not one step can be skipped over. There are valuable life lessons that has to be learned on every step, because if you lack spiritual maturity your gift will get you in the door but it won't keep you there. A person's gift may get them in the position they desire but their ungodly character will get them kicked right out the door. God wants us to mature and grow up in the things of the spirit. Proving that you are true, trustworthy and watch our awesome God pour you out a blessing that you won't have room enough to receive. Are you being a good steward over the things that God has given you? He has more! bigger things to place in your hands. God wants to know from his people will you do what is right with what I have entrusted you with? Meditate on your answer before you air it out of your mouth . God will never prosper a person more than what they can handle. He knows what will literally destroy us and draw us away from Him. Prove yourself responsible and mature right where you are, so you can experience the fullness of heavens best right here on earth.....

John 1:15:5, *"I am the vine, ye are the branches. He that abideth in me, and I in him the same bringeth forth much fruit."* For without me ye can do nothing. God does the fertilizing so we can produce much fruit but we are going to have to stay connected to the vine (Jesus Christ). If we disconnect from our life support we die out while wondering in the wilderness never reaching our true potential. If God doesn't give you the ability, talent, grace and power to do what you do you couldn't do anything. Do you have the mustard seed faith in what you are saying? The things you are speaking out of your mouth are going to bring forth a harvest in your life. Whatever you are continually saying will be multiplied in your life. Sometimes we believe with our mouths and doubt in our hearts. With the heart God says we are to believe and with our mouth confession is made. The words you speak will determine the future you will have. Why pray for something that you really don't have the faith to believe for? Faith requires a corresponding action from you. It is literally a waste of time if you only say and do nothing, right? Of course it is. God responds too our faith not our need. So he gives us seed which is the word of God. Learn how to target your need with a seed and watch God put our enemy to shame. Also, learn the importance of being a giver instead of having your hand held out waiting on the mercy of other people to sustain you. As you practice the principle of giving you show forth the ways of our Father. He gave us His only son that we may live in abundance and have eternal life. How many people will give up the only thing in their life that is of significant value to them? No one will that's why God displayed the first act of selfless love by giving His only son. The most selfless act humanity has ever experienced. The Lord did this as an example for all humanity to act and follow. When you don't know who you are and what your rights are as a delegated authority, as an heir of God, you will begin to give up more to gain the attention of other people, and live beneath your privileges as a child of God. The enemy will arrest your mind, hijack your thoughts and gain advantage over you because of what you don't know. Only to keep you living in the land of lack hindering you from experiencing the land of plenty. Making it merely impossible to do what our Father has called and predestined us to do. Because you're so focused on all the messes that are in your present moment instead of focusing on where you're going. When I received the Lord in my own life it was a struggle for me to receive what God said I could have. The battle between my spirit and my mind was real. The voices in our head is in great opposition to our spirit that fights the knowledge of God in our heart. After all, I didn't have my biological father in my home to aim and steer me to the Lord. However, God gave me a loving, nurturing, caring and praying mother. Constantly, I use to ask myself how can God bless me with so much and why does He even want to after all that I have done wrong in my life? Daily I had to meditate on the word of God and fill my mind with the scriptures about everything that God said I was and what I could have. Then deplete what other's had said to me, about me, and spoken over me that didn't line up with the word of God. The rhema word I pulled out of the logos, and applied it to my circumstances so I could begin the process of reconditioning my mind to the spiritual things of God. If you are struggling to believe God the enemy will make sure labels and stigmas from other's will stick to you like superglue paralyzing your thinking to hinder you from reaching fulfillment and success. No one has to teach us how to be destructive, wasteful, irresponsible and everything else that is lawless because we were born in sin and shapened in iniquity. The rebellion and sinful nature of Adam and Eve when they ate from the tree of knowledge of good and evil caused our minds to be at war with the spirit of God. God said don't eat of the tree and the voice of the enemy beguiled them both to eat creating a war in both worlds. Causing man to struggle with whether they should obey God or justify why they shouldn't. Impregnating a woman with the spirit of manipualtion to seduce authority and planting the seed of rebellion in man to lean on his own understanding and not God's. When did obeying the voice of God become optional? Being taught how to think right and how to be productive is the process that's most complicated for most people. The average person does things without thinking. Personally, I was one of those people. Operating in the systems of this world verses operating in the kingdom principles was quite different as I too had to be taught, and we all are forever learning. Thank God for his grace. A person just has to have a desire to grow and want to know God on a deeper and more intimate level. This is what it means to hunger and thirst for righteousness. Discipline, having a desire and diligence should become your new best friend right now. Make that choice today. The kingdom of God's principle says *"give and it shall be given unto you."* The world system says *"Get, or injure to get whatever you want"* and *"an eye for and eye."* God tells us to pray for those who hate us and despitefully use us. When you constantly stay in the word of God you will gain spiritual muscles, as you practice by living out what you are reading. Realizing as you are dealing with the wiles of your enemy applying godly solutions to every problem will become easy for you to emulate because you will be exercising your spiritual mind and not being led by the carnal mind.

The most reassuring part of all of this is you will begin to see the desired result, and this is what causes your faith to grow. When you choose the worlds way of doing things, and conform to their standard of living, and thinking it will always leave you depleted, disappointed, disconnected and in lack. Living by the word of God is the best prescription for success in a persons life if positive results are the desired outcome. Now you are on the path of enlightenment, productivity, fruitbearing, soul winning and increase. Then and only then will our Lord be glorified. Simply because when He looks down from heaven at His creation increasing, expanding, learning and producing He sees Himself. We are now imitating the Father. When God looks in the mirror of our life He is looking for a reflection of Himself. That's why God orchestrates storms, situations and circumstances in our life so we can become more like Him. The problems were sent to help us not so that we can question our value and self- worth. God has more confidence in what He put in you than you do. That's one of the main reasons He sometimes doesn't rush to pull you out. Change your perception about whatever you are going through because how you perceive a thing will determine if you will experience defeat or walk in victory. How do you see yourself? Where did that thought come from? Are you thinking things are too bad to get better? Are you in the fiery furnace right now? If all demonic warfare has broken loose in your life that means you're in a trial of fire before embarking on the promotion of a lifetime. Elevation will always come after persecution. God wants us to exercise our own power, authority, and not feel as if we are inadequate and powerless. Are your kids going too the left? Is your spouse telling you to curse God and die? If God has allowed the storm in your life to blow like he did Job. He is obligated to bring you out with double for your trouble. Fire is a refiner and an element used to remove all the impurities from your soul. So whenever you miss the mark and aren't producing fruit, display arrogance, cockiness, prideful behavior, enviousness and jealousy God throws us right back in the fire to be purified. Don't think this process is a quick fix because it's not. God keeps us in this place until He is pleased and when He can see a reflection of Himself in us. Now don't go and keep getting yourself in messes thinking and expecting God to get you out. This is taking the mercy of God for granted. You've been down this road before. God got you out of this crazy relationship and you've put yourself right back in it knowing this person is no good for you. Now here you are pleading with God to get you out again. Lord, I know what this feels like because I was in this disempowering cycle of unhealthy relationships too but I was sick and tired of ending up in the same place. A place called *"No Where"* that I had conditioned myself to being in by choosing what I had always chosen. We will always attract the people that mirror our dysfunction when we are not healed from emtional baggage and trauma. A cycle of toxicity and co-dependency. I've hit a fork in the road again. Only to plead and ask God yet again for forgiveness, and promising him yet again I'll get out of your way for real this time and let you be Lord of my life. We suffer so much privately while putting on a brave face publicly only masking the pain that goes deep within the soul. When you go through enough trouble and pain in your life you will eventually get sick and tired of yourself and mean what you're praying to God about. Prayer changes us and transforms our thinking. At this point in the process of deliverance you aren't going back to the past for nothing. As children of God we have a greater responsiblity to those who are walking in darkness that have no revelation knowledge of the father. When God gave me revelation of his unconditional love for me I began to repent of everything in my life that the holy spirit brought back to my remembrance. Boy did I weep and beg the father for forgiveness and mercy. From that moment on God forever changed my life and gave me spiritual direction to fulfill my divine assignment. I had an encounter with God that left me broken but whole at the same time. Weights, chains, strongholds, unhealthy soul ties, wrong thinking and burdens fell off of me. Things that I had tolerated in the past literally caused me to now frown upon. Other people's opinion of me was of no concern of mine anymore. Thank God for freeing me and redeeming my life from destruction and crowning me with his lovingkindness and tender mercies. The Lord began to use me prophetically, with words of knowledge, wisdom, and revelation to minister to his people. Self- Forgiveness and Self-Love is powerful and liberating. Also God gave me a greater love and compassion for his people, and for the things that concerned the Kingdom of God. Fruit bearing became an evident witness to my call and office as a prophetess. By way of the precious Holy Spirit with demonstration. Be faithful right where you are and watch God increase you more and more.

1. Honor God with the First-Fruits of everything
2. Be a giver and not just a receiver
3. Display true repententance with action
4. Pray in Faith
5. Hear, Listen, and Obey God in all things
6. Don't be afraid to be controversial
7. Always give God the glory

No matter where you are right now in your life start being productive by being intentional when creating the life you desire. If you are faithful in a few things God will make you ruler over many. Did you know that it is never too late to succeed in life when it comes to God? That means you haven't messed up bad enough that the Heavenly Father won't forgive you and help you get to your desired place in life. The enemy sure wants you to think it's to late. God is for us and not against us. Please keep this saying before you the rest of your life because this is going to determine where you end up in life while on the journey that God has assigned you to be. The devil is against us that's why he is always trying to plant seeds of fear, doubt, loneliness, faithlessness and insecurity in our thought process. The enemy is after the knowledge you know and don't know that pertains to the truth of the spoken word of God. The measure of your success is in the stability of your mind, and the quality of the life you'll experience is determined by how much word you have, and apply to your battles. If the enemy of your thoughts can get humanity to think contrary to God then he can penetrate your faith in the word of God. The war in the soul has begun and the enemy knows that God only deal with faith not suggestion. He wants you to be confused and unsure about your birthright. Remember as a man thinketh in his heart so is he. It's really true. If you think you can't you won't. If you think you're nothing, you will become nothing and everyone that you come in contact with will pick up on that negative, low-vibrational energy and treat you as such. Your adversary would like nothing more for you to allow these negative thoughts and emotions to stay parked in your head. Your life will be a self-fulfilling prophecy that you've rehearsed. Did you know that even the thoughts that you are thinking this very moment while reading this book are seeds? Keeping God's own creation at odds with Him by doubt and disbelief is the enemies prayer. The devil is a liar. The father of lies. There will never be any truth in him so why allow him to get your spirit man in turmoil. We already know the tactics of the enemy. He wants to conquer, kill, steal, destroy and divide. Don't you allow the devil to take up residence in your mind and trick you out of all the beautiful things that God has spoken over your life. To have and enjoy so that you will be a blessing to other people and bear witness of the Lord Jesus Christ. Developing a prayer life is essential in our walk with God. No prayer life means a defeated and a depleted life. Having a prayer life means having a life of power and the ability to walk out what God says you can have while doing it in the spirit of excellence. Prayer in the life of a true believer is an act of total assurance and confidence in the plan and purpose of God. In Luke 11:24 and Matt. 6:9-13, Jesus set an example for us to pray. His entire lifestyle was based on prayer and sometimes isolating himself having that alone time with the Father. Jesus stayed connected to His Father and that's how He was able to produce much fruit, do miracles having signs and wonders following Him. We aren't exempt. We are trying to do things that God has called us to do without prayer and some of us are doing things that God has not called us to do without a prayer life as well. The enemy knows the word of God and the power of prayer and praise. It's your responsiblity to know the word. Satan was a worshipper in heaven that had instruments built within him, to sing praises, to give glory and honor to God. The enemy of the soul will let you do things in your own strength in hopes to tire you out so you won't reach your full potential in life, knowing you will never become the person that God called you to be. Pray with faith in the name of Jesus. The Prayer of Faith discerns Gods will an acts as a preserver until what you have prayed for comes to pass. Never do anything without seeking God through prayer and through His word. Rid yourselves of all unforgiveness and offenses with others because this will hinder your prayers from being heard first and of course they will not be answered. You will be talking about the things God has called and showed you but there will be no manifestation of the vision, blessings, provisions or miracles. So many of us think we can violate the principles of God and get the blessings of God. The devil is a liar. My desire is for you to win in life while destroying the kingdom of darkness by applying the principles in the word. But let me warn you the more you start believing, working the word, decreeing and professing it. The enemy sets out to sabotage you and everyone that's connected to you in your life. Just remember that this too shall pass. The song says trouble doesn't last always. When the storms of life begin raging hold on to God's unchanging hand. Be relentless and let the adversary know I don't care what circumstance you send my way God is bigger than it all. If God be for me who can be against me and win? After all, He made the storm and God will still make himself known to His people if He has to do it in a pillar of cloud by day or a pillar of fire by night. Even if you find yourself between a rock and a hard place just like the children of Israel did when they were coming out of bondage in Egypt. Stand still and see the salvation of the Lord. God will part the Red Sea for you as He leads you into safe waters allowing you to watch the demise of your enemies. Whatever the father has to do to get you to the place where He has promised you He will. All God requires us to do is to trust Him and take Him at His word. Is it hard to trust a God who has never lost a battle? There is no if God will deliver you because He said He would and God keeps His word. God is not a man that He should lie nor the son of man that He should repent; and then say *"I'm sorry I changed my mind today about delivering you."* Trust in the mighty hand of God and in His deliverance. God didn't bring you this far so the enemy could wipe you out and destroy you. Come on people you know the devil will never win when it comes to God. If this was true Lucifer, His angels would have exalted the throne of the most high God. You and I both know that this will never ever be a dilemma for God. Go through every test and trial of life that opposes your destiny. So when you come out you'll come out as pure gold to do the masters will. For all the world to behold your divine nature as they witness your productivity and fruitfulness. The hearts of others will be encouraged in their very own season of adversity and testing after hearing, knowing and seeing you as a living testimony come out victorious on the other side. Many are the afflictions of the righteous but God will deliver us out of them all. If we don't suffer as the Lord we can't reign in the Kingdom of God. So focus on being like Christ even in times of suffering. It's through our pain and suffering that a greater anointing is birthed, which will enable you to become more fruitful and productive creating the life you desire while bringing glory to our Father. As you are one with infinite intelligence, the creator of all things, God.

CHAPTER SIX

"MIRRORING AND HEALING EMOTIONAL TRAUMA"

❖❖❖❖❖

Have you ever attracted people in your life that betrayed you, rejected you, dropped you, played mind games, emotionally disconnected, and wore a mask during the duration of the friendship/relationship? Bringing you to the conclusion that you were the only one being authentic, realizing they despised you for the favor of God on your life, they slandered your name and reputation, then treated you far less than the beautiful soul that God created you to be? Have you endured crisis after crisis? Are you a magnet for people that are broken, lost, down on their luck, always needing something from you and never making an equal investment in your life finding their way to you? Then after you serve the purpose for their need they are gone from your life until the next episode. Do you have a problem telling others no? Are you overcompensating and getting little or nothing in return from the people you're investing in? If so this is what I have personally defined as *"The Self- Mirroring Effect."* It places a maginifying glass on those inner child trauma's that we've not yet been healed from. There is a reason why this is happening to you. God is forcing change by pushing all this pain to the surface in your life because you didn't get what he was trying to teach you. It happens to all of God's children, and when you can understand and focus on why it happened instead of what happened the healing in your soul comes sooner rather than later. These are lessons that God wants us to learn from and experiences that He wants us to have because it teaches us so much that we couldn't perceive as we self-sabotage ourselves. This magnifying glass reveals to us why our life hasn't been working up to this point. It also helps us to comprehend the blame we've placed on others should be placed on ourselves as well because it's always easier to blame someone else for your shortcomings, rather than take the repsonsibility and put the required effort in to change your own life. Blaming others requires no action for change and transformation. Never question nor personalize the poor treatment that a person gives you because it's a self-reflection of their inner wounds, abandonment issues, and brokenness that they need to be healed from themselves. At this moment and time, that individual doesn't have the capacity to give you whatever it is you're desiring. It forces us to confront the issues we have purposely hidden due to past hurts that were caused from the people that were suppose to love us, nurture us and protect us. Pain causes you to self-reflect in a healthy aspect when you're desiring to be the greatest version of who you are as a child of God. The primary goal is to take away the knowledge you have now gained from each painful experience and soar freely in this world like a beautiful butterfly. You have now transformed or are in the process of transforming into the spiritual person that God created you to be while being molded on the potters wheel. Forgive others as quick as they hurt you instead of finding a reason to hold a grudge. Forgiving those that have hurt you is for you and not for those who have betrayed you. As they have truly betrayed themselves. Release the traumas that people have caused you and let God give you justice against those who have hurt you, took from you and didn't think twice about it. Trust me He will, and when that time comes you will be so unfazed by it, because your soul has healed causing the trajectory of your life to take you to places you've once imagined. The time has come for you to release, purge and heal what no longer serves your life so you can make a mark in this world that can't be erased. Leave the past behind you even if people don't offer you an apology. However, accept their apology if it's given and move forward without them. Forgiving a person that betrayed you doesn't mean you have to be reconciled to them. It means I'm taking back my power, my self-worth, dignity, value and walking into my future healed in my spirit, soul and body. Make a decision to forgive even if you don't feel like it. I want to encourage you to go get a piece of paper and write a letter to all the people who have hurt you. Offer your forgiveness to them, then throw it in a fire pit to burn, never to re-live it, never to rehearse it in your mind or in your day to day conversations. People who genuinely love you will most definitely love you with all of your flaws, when you've messed up, made the wrong decision, having a bad hair day or a good one. Although this is a lonely and painful process to endure just know that in order for any of us to reach our highest God given potential knowledge, and pain has to be a part of our experience so we can grow, evolve and expand in this world. Which means we will at times be exposed to things and people in this world that will hurt us that doesn't have our best interest at heart. Tests will be given and the lessons from them must be learned or you will repeat the cycle in another season of your life. I must warn you that while you're going through the mirroring effect feelings of disbelief, sadness, mere shock, regret, anger and bitterness will be brought to the surface so that the true heart of a person is revealed to you by God. As the conditions of your own heart will be placed under a microscope to bring about healing from all the issues that are hindering your personal success. The spiritual path to awakening and renewal that you're embarking on is purposeful and the time has come for you to cut out any and all unhealthy soul ties, attachments and cords. The people that you have had connections with throughout the years end the emotional contract you gave them to your soul has to be severed because they came to your life to teach you valuable life lessons on forgiveness, having the courage to release what doesn't serve your life for the greatest good, how to set healthy boundaries in all relationships, what equal give and take is, the importance of self love if we are to receive true love in this world, and etc. Have you ever taken an inventory of your belief system? Why you believe what you believe? Do these beliefs come from you? Or have you been influenced to believe what you believe from someone else? Like your surroundings, the media or your peers, etc? Watch what you say and monitor how you think and feel as you are creating circumstances that will mirror your every word. The average person finds it difficult to believe and admit that where they are in life right now is their own fault regardless of what family we come from and what environment we were born in . Someone else is always at fault for what's going on in their life or the lack there of. No matter where God has placed us, He has given us a way of escape and it's really unfortunate that most of us have been brainwashed to look to others for all the help we need instead of looking to God first then going within ourselves. As some people also believe your words have little to no effect on what's transpiring in their life right now. They credit it to just mere bad luck or that's their normal. If this is your belief system you will find yourself hitting a wall of opposition and resistance instead of allowing abundance to flow freely and effortlessly into your life in an easy and natural way. The way that God designed it to be from the very beginning. Haven't you spoken what you don't want out loud in the atmosphere only to get all the things that you didn't want? The average person does this by default not even considering they will eat the fruit of their words. Watch what you say. Death and life are in the power of the tongue. Your words are like a boomerang bringing back to you what you have sent out. Mirroring what is projecting from within you into your current reality. What you give out must come back to you. Words don't die they become life when you open your mouth and speak. This is a Universal Law (Galatians 6). So why is that? This is how God chose for us to be governed as we operate in His kingdom. Have you programmed your mind to believe that the only way that you can acquire wealth and financial freedom is through a job, hard work and endless effort? Do you believe there are no honest and loyal people in the world? Or nobody can really be happy in every area of their life? If so these are called belief blockages that influences how a person has conditioned their mind to think about succeeding by what their reality for success looks like for them in their own mind. Our up bringing can take a first seat to this dysfunction. We all have been programmed by the belief system's of other people growing up no matter what place they share in our life. For example your parents may have told you going to college upon graduating from high school is out of the question, because no one else in the family has a college degree, or there's no money so just apply for a job that pays good. So many choices we make or don't make are highly influenced by the people in our life. So what is your belief system? What percentage of what you really believe comes from you? What have you programmed your mind to believe? Are you meditating on the thoughts of the things you want? Who and what has shaped what you currently believe? What conclusions are you thinking and saying about yourself and others? You have to deprogram your mind because what you believe, think and feel shapes your life. And we attract to us who we are on the inside and we can thank our limiting belief system for that. This is an enemy of our faith. If it's something you want to change in your life pick up the remote control and change the channel. Staying stuck in any situation is a choice. If you're unfulfilled and unhappy with the movie that's broadcasting on the screen of your mind change it. You are the writer and the producer of your life and whatever gains your attention becomes your reality. It's imperative that we learn how to become deliberate thinker's and deliberate focusers. Your mind is like a television or radio station that operates from different levels of frequencies but remember you can only focus on one frequency at a time. For example, if you want to listen to jazz music you can't be tuned in on a classical music station as the two frequencies are different. It's the same for your thoughts. You can't speak healing scripture's and in your mind doubt that you're going to be healed. You must focus on one channel at a time and vibrate on that particular frequency. So whatever you are believing for focus on that while making sure you're feeling positive, happy, joyful and emotions of gratitude. The next time you open your mouth to speak you'll come from a place of faith and positivity because you've built up the inner man. Giving evidence to yourself that you are divinely aligned with God creating the life you were always intended to live from the space of eternity.

The Spirit of the Lord is life, peace, fullness and wholeness in the lives of all humanity. Therefore, it really doesn't matter how bad of a place or situation a person is in it only takes one word to leave your mouth and change your life forever. So, never think that where you are right now is all that you will become nor think this is the place that you will remain. Things will get better and they have a way of working out for my good should be said on a daily basis. Tell yourself this and erradicate all limiting beliefs and blockages. It's a temporary situation that is subject to change. This is not your permanent zipcode. Go ahead and start prophesying over whatever you want to change. When Lazarus was dead and stinking in his grave Jesus said *"Lazarus come forth,"* and a dead man wrapped up and bound in burial clothing came walking out of his tomb. His faith was not needed nor required only the power of the spoken word. Which is called the *"rhema word"* it's where we pull out a kingdom principle from the word of God and apply it to our situation. Secondly, when God created the world and it was void and without form the father started saying *"let there be and it was."* When darkness comprehended the light from coming forth our God said *"let there be light,"* and there was. Don't you understand how powerful the spoken word of God is? Words from the spirit of God will bring healing to negative thought patterns, beliefs, disempowering cycles of your soul and in every situation in your life. Anytime we talk about the spirit of God we're talking about the very essence of God Himself. Job said *"the breath of the almighty has given me life."* God's word is medicine to our afflicted souls. David said *"his word is a lamp unto my feet and a light unto my pathway."* That's why nothing should be done in our lives or in our churches until the spirit speaks and moves on behalf of that circumstance. The spirit of God will not always strive with man the word of God tells us. Stay mindful when God impresses upon your heart to do things and go places as He is requiring us to act immediately so that the task is accomplished. If the spirit of God is trying to get you to another level and you keep making excuses like *"I will do it later"* and *"I have time to do it tomorrow"* God will politely get out of our way and let us do things our way and in our own strength with no prevail. It is so important to know and to be able to learn and discern the Spirit of God so that we don't miss out on Gods best for our life. Our first reaction should not always be to consult with a mere person then God as the last option. Yes, I agree with getting professional help as some cases will need the immediate attention of that medical professional. I am not discouraging anyone from seeking help nor am I encouraging or advising you not to. Always do as you are led as I am not a medical professional so use your own discretion. Trusting God and making Him the priority and not just an option is my focal point even as you treat with doctor's as I had to as well. It's not until words of the spirit of God are spoken over you, your minsitry, business, family, health, spouse, children, finances, and future that you will see the change and the results that you are hoping and praying for that helps us to understand when someone speaks negative words to you and over you it sticks to you like glue. Immediately, you must cancel ill spoken word curses, cast down all vain imaginations that tries to exalt itself against the knowledge of God. The enemy comes to attack the truth that we know about God and His promises to us. I remember when I was young and growing up as a child I would so bodly say *"sticks and stones may break my bones but words will never hurt me."* That was so untrue because alot of those negative words that was said to me rolled over to my early years, then into my adulthood and it took the power of the Holy Spirit to wash every negative word curse that people had said to me, against me and about me out of mind. Causing me during those dark times in my soul to question myself, my value, my worth and spiritual gifts. When words leave our mouth they take shape and form into positive or negative things. As much as possible be mindful of what you're thinking and speaking during the day. As we walk closer with the Lord, He will teach us how to deal with all of the garbage that some of us have gone through. Don't go around superficially saying *"yes, that happened to me when I was young and it has no affect of who I am today."* I beg to differ. If the Holy Spirit has not purged you then there is still some residue within you just waiting on an opportuned time to come out. Let's get real and honest so we can be delivered and healed for real. If God delivers you from a situation and you haven't been healed from the condition there is a huge possibility that you're going back to the dysfunction that in your mind is normal. When we go to God we have to go to Him in all honesty and in all truth. Trying to be impressive with God is a waste of time as it shows a person is not really ready for the change that is needed for them to thrive in life. Obedience and faith with action impresses God to move on your behalf and nothing else. As

God is a spirit and not flesh. The Lord is patiently waiting on us to ask Him for His help and to let Him know how messed up and tore up from the floor up we really are. He already knows the truth. Remember, He created you and has also reminded us that open confession is good for the soul. Keep in mind that the sin you are desperately trying to hide is like a malignant cancer spreading and eating away at you down to the marrow in your bones. God is waiting on us to confront our issues instead of covering them up with cosmetics. What can one conceal from God? God knows your thoughts before you even think them and scripture goes on to tell us that He has numbered each strand of hair on our heads. God just wants us to acknowledge where we are and depend on Him. Religion, our culture and our teachings that we have been pre-exposed to from our childhood has messed alot of us up. This proves that there is a battle going on with the spirit man and with our flesh. When we come to the Lord and when we begin to read and study His word resistance and opposition makes an appearance in the face of our faith. Old ways of thinking will revert right back to the teachings we have received growing up until we make a decision to start deleting all this bad information so we can start winning in life. Are you comparing the word of God to the teachings you were taught before being born again? Does what you currently believe line up with the word of God? Are you now talking like it? This is a process and it takes time so don't rush yourself. Each and everyday do what God has told you to do by renewing your mind through the word on a daily basis. Meditate on it day and night. Calm your mind and allow yourself to be so consumed with what God says about you until it's not even funny. I mean everytime life tells you you can't do something bodly open up your mouth and tell the enemy what God said you can have, what you will become and who you are as a child of God. At this point in time you definitely can't afford to be silent when the devil is bodly in your face talking a bunch of nonsense. It's going to ultimately come down to you making a decision as to whose report you will believe in. As for me and my house, we choose to believe the report of the living God. Is there anything to hard for the Lord to do? Of course not. Think of how big the smile will be on God's face when hHe sees His creation speaking the word in faith, in corresponding action, with a fierce boldness in the face of adversity and in the midst of all your enemies. You talking about the Father hurrying up to rescue you and showing out to let your enemies know whose still favored. I release you right now in the name of Jesus to speak words of life over everything in your life that is dead, dying, unfruitful, barren and watch what happens. You can't operate in the spirit of fear and receive the promises. The devil knows if you are operating in the spirit of fear you are held captive like an inmate in a prison cell but the difference is your prison walls are self created by you. Always operate in the realm of faith in the midst of the storms of life. Faith in Gods word is what's going to release change and multiplication in our lives nothing else is going to do it. Just sitting by and saying I'm going to wait on God to speak to me is a no no. God has already told you what to do in the word. So act on it. It's not enough for us to say I believe what the word says then do nothing to prove our faith. It's when we put our faith and belief into action that shows God that we believe in him and in every word that we have spoken. After all the word is God. The word was with God in the beginning and without Him there was not anything made that was made. Create your own life by the words that come out of your mouth. Never speak anything that you don't want to receive fruit from. Alot of people that I have had the pleasure of ministering to could not even perceive how they could speak a thing and it would be. It was only after they got a better understanding of the word of God through developing a deeper and more personal relationship with the father that showed them how powerful their words are and have been the entire time. Your life right now is a result of the thoughts you have thought, the words you have spoken and the emotions you feel. If you speak negative words over a situation day after day why would you expect to receive a positive result? It's ignorant to think this way. Speak words of life over your circumstance and watch it change for the better. Relinquish yourself from trying to figure out how in the world God is going to do what he said he was going to do for you and just know that he is. Personally, I use to struggle with this so bad and it use to stress me out that I couldn't sleep very well. I would get depressed and very irritable because I was trying to figure God out. Give me the details God so I can go to bed. Until one day God spoke very softly to my spirit *"It's your job to only believe me and it's my job to do what I said."* Yes that is the truth. I started to think on what the Holy Spirit said to me and I released everything to the father because I learned not to care how God was going to do what he promised me and I started saying I know you will even though I don't know when or how you are going to do it. I do know that you will. This is The Law Of Trusting And Allowing. After all, whatever vision that God has shown you it's his job to fund it and make it happen. Our only job is to trust what he said and obey Him nothing less or nothing more. The frustration with the promises and vision God shows you is He doesn't show you the scenes in the middle. This leads to frustration because you can't fill in the blanks of how it's going to happen, when, where, why and who. That part is none of your business your business is to walk by faith acting as if you have the manifestation of the promise already. God only showed you where you would end up right? And let me guess where you are right now doesn't even look like where God showed you. I have been there and done that. This is your valley experience and every person that God anoints, appoints, calls and chooses has to go through this hard place because God has to get out everything that will hinder us from being successful when we get to our *"Canaan"* The Land of Promise. Especially an *"Egypt And Slave Mentality"* one who thinks they have to beg to eat. Or the one who believe's they have to settle for whatever life so happens to give them. Prepared people get the blessing. It doesn't matter how much you think you are ready. God will always allow you to go through a battle to strengthen you and to show you that you may think that you're ready but you aren't. You still get and attitude when people don't speak to you and when they over look you. You think people are the one who provides for you and open doors of opportunity for you. God uses people according to what he desires to accomplish in your life according to his own will. We are not the center of attention. The death, burial and resurrection of our Lord is the main feature and hot topic. If by any chance you've made this mistake take yourself off of this pedistal that people have possibly put you on, or God will. We are puppets in the hands of our God. He's the puppet master behind the stage pulling the strings in our life. And we are at His mercy in case you didn't know that. God has allowed all of these experiences to visit your life so He can pour fresh oil in you to be frutiful, to bring multiplication in our lives, and bring glory and honor to His name. Our number one priority should only be for us to be about our Father's business. Yes, I know God called you to do a great thing in the earth but you better keep yourself humble and know that it still isn't about you or me. Just be honored that God loved you enough that He chose you for such a time as this. We all have a part to play and whatever role the Father has designated for you accept it and get the job done. It's not going to change and every second counts, every minute and every day counts. You're running out of time. Our life is like a vapor. It's here today and it may be gone tomorrow. Personally, I'm not going to die prematurely, nor do I want to stand before my maker without accomplishing what I was predestined to do. I will die empty. God is going to judge us on everything. I mean everything. We are going to be without excuse. Please get alone with the Father and seek him while he may be found and ask God *"why am I here, and what would you have me to do."* Don't you want to reach your maximum potential while you are here in this world? Don't you want to be all that you desire to be? Yes, I know you do and God wants that more than you want that for yourself. That's hard to hear and believe isn't it? I know it is because I felt the same way before the holy-spirit got a hold of me. I use to think how can God want me to be more successful than I want to be successful myself? Jeremiah 29:11(KJV) says, *"I know the thoughts that I think toward you, saith the Lord, thoughts of peace, and not of evil, to give you and expected end."* Now take God at His word and meditate on it day and night until you start thinking and dreaming about what God has shown you. When you do that you will find yourself proclaiming, declaring and decreeing what the word of the Lord says. Most importantly, you're going to feel amazing. Now start believing God for bigger and better things in your life not just to get your car payment paid, a light bill and gas in the car. How about believing God to bless you so that you can fund the Kingdom of God, build homeless shelters and camps for the youth that have been abused and abandoned, etc.

The heart is vital to what and how much the Lord can entrust to His people because alot of people do the right thing for the wrong reason. Your heart is the second compartment of your mind. It's the seat of your affections. Motives are very important to God because they too are an issue that dwells within the heart. Some people give to get instead of giving out of a place of love. Do a daily inventory of your heart before you ask God for anything and before you do a good deed for someone else. Think about this what if you had a neighbor and you knew they were in need. You realized that your neighbor had kids that didn't have clothes, shoes and food to eat and you never took it upon yourself to sow a seed in the life of that family.

One Sunday morning there's a guest speaker at your church and the pastor tells the entire congregation how the speaker and his family are in need and have driven many miles to deliver the word of God to the congregation, and the pastor asks for a volunteer to take care of the family and take care of any needs they may have. And without hesitation you are the first person to raise your hand. But why? What would be the motive? I totally support helping but what about the neighbor that you see everyday and you never helped. God never brought conviction in your heart to help them? James 2:15 NIV says, suppose a brother or sister is without clothes and daily food. If one of you says to him *"Go, I wish you well; keep warm and well fed,"* but does nothing about his physical needs. As children of God we have an obligation to feed peoples souls, and we do that through preaching this life changing message of our Lord and our saviour Jesus Christ. We have stickers on our cars, on our bibles, we wear WWJD bracelets but why are we doing these things if we don't represent the person (Jesus Christ) with inspired action? If some people aren't careful the devil is going to snatch alot of them right into lake of fire. Let me tell you something about our enemy. He doesn't care how many times we go to church, how much we sing in the choir nor does he care about our testimony services. The enemy wants people to continue to go to the house of God faking, lacking in their love walk and in disobedience so they can burn in hells bottomless pit with him and his angels. Aren't you aware that every time the enemy sees believers *"playing church"* he accuses them before our Father? The devil is afraid of people who have a real, and intimate relationship with God because we have the power to destroy him and his entire camp. Then he realizes we have found our true identity as a believer. Get on the right team so every demon will know whose side you're really on. When the devil hears you praying words of the spirit, walking in humility and obedience to God he gets nervous, angry and afraid. Not only is he trembling he is getting his paper and pen out drawing and devising new strategies on how to defeat the people of God. He can't stand the fact of how our speech, heart and faith is aligned with that of God. The devil is always thinking of ways on how he can destroy a persons life. So never lay your sword down and think that you can rest because you have defeated the enemy. He is a defeated foe but remember he wants to wear the saints of God out through adversities and through the storms of life. The war may be over but there will still be some battles to fight. We have a great responsibility and a God to glorify as we live out our life here on earth. The word is always the answer. Speak the word of God over your circumstances and be confident in knowing that the Lord will bring His word to pass in His timing. Remember wherever the word of God is spoken there will be positive change because they are words of the spirit that brings life, healing, positive transformation and restoration to every area of your life. You are a magnet that draws everything into your present experience. Feeling worthy is an important component for you to receive what God said is already yours as you are the mirror of God's reflection throughout the span of time......

"THE POWER OF THOUGHTS AND EMOTIONS"

Every person that wants to experience the promises of God must learn and master the art of becoming a *"deliberate thinker"* as well as master their emotions of feeling good even when bad things come to shift their current reality, because thought and emotions shapes the destiny of a persons life. As the heart is the birthing canal to where all things are to come to fruition in your life. It is the seat of our emotion's and it's where all the issues of life stem from. Guard your heart with all diligence, and monitor what you allow to enter into the heart space of your soul. God's ear is inclined to his righteous seed who are fervently praying from a broken and contrite spirit. We believe with our heart and not with our brain. Balance has to be brought to both before the windfalls of abundace invades our life. This is done by reprograming the old software that is in your subconscious mind causing the new system (The word of God) that is now in place to eliminate all old thought patterns, memories, images and the emotions that come with them that has hindered you from having successful relationships with your spouse, children, family, friends, co-workers, etc. Your subconscious mind (where stored ideas are) is like a field where seeds (thoughts) are planted and sown. As a farmer tends to his field (mind) on a regular basis to ensure the soil (heart) is healthy, and is getting enough water for proper nourishment, while pulling up weeds (doubt) that has the potential to threaten the health of the crop (represents your life). You must do the same thing when it comes to your thought life and your emotions. Our subconscious mind helps us to remember things we've previously learned. For example, the first time we read a book or rode a bicycle. It is literally a file cabinet that holds all of our experiences. And when something or someone triggers a past emotion, past hurt our subconscious mind quickly reminds us of the feeling that was associated with that experience. It has a great impact on how we behave on a day to day basis. However, our conscious mind is where we use our senses on a day to day basis that allows us to reason, make assumptions, receive or reject information. Your subconsious mind does not have the liberty to choose what it will believe or accept because it operates from a place of pre-programmed habits that governs how and what we believe. When you remain consistent in exercising the power of daily repetition, thinking and speaking *"I Am"* and *"I Have"* affirmations, this will propel you right into the life you've always wanted in divine timing. This process is going to assist you in reconditioning the mind to create, and provoke positive changes along with building healthy belief systems, as you are now awakened to who you are as a child of the most high God. Now you have the clarity that is needed so you can make the proper distinctions in your life. As we establish positive experiences in our life it causes new and profound belief's to remove what no longer serves the inner man. Let the new cycles begin. However, Let's not forget *"Visualization"* and the importance of being specific as possible while writing down (Hab.2:2) exactly what you want *"the vision"* to be as you learn to hold the picture of the promise in your imagination. You are exercising your will to focus (mental faculty). This is going to help you master your emotions as you continue to focus on what you want. It's possible to have physical sight but no vision. Secondly, you can also create a vision board as a tool for you to meditate on and be specific as possible when it comes to writing down what you are believing God for. Now close your eyes as you visualize how you look thriving in your own company and how does it feel to have what you are believing for even before it shows up in your life? Find the good feeling of that positive emotion and rest in the momemtum of it, and the blessing will seek to find you instead of you looking for it. How will you help others when you receive whatever it is you have been praying for? Make sure your motives are coming from a place of love, and authenticity because God is not into blessing anyone for the purpose of self-gratification, to prove a point to the people that hurt us. One of the main reasons why I think people are not getting what God has promised them is because they're constantly processing athoughts of disbelief, rehearsing the pains of the past, complaining and not being grateful for what they do have in the current moment. They are constantly having an unhealthy, internal dialogue telling themselves over and over again why they can't have what God said they can have. This is a pointless argument that makes no logical sense, which will only hinder you from receiving what you really want, because you are perceiving your problems as limitations and not seeing the opportunity for God to prove himself faithful in that bad situation. In other words, you are looking from the eyes of the physical and not that which is spiritual. If you can see it that means it's temporal and subject to change, and if you can't see it you are looking from the eye's of the spirit which is eternal. Remember whatever thoughts and emotions you are sending out from within yourself life is going to create more of those circumstances and experiences to validate what you've asked for from the heart. As your heart has a voice so be mindful of whatever frequency you are vibrating on and resonating with as it will definitely manifest in your life's experiences. Only allow your thoughts to vibrate on the frequency you want to receive in your life, because it's difficult and nearly impossible for the mind to properly focus on more than one station at a time. You need to understand the importance of bringing stability to your mind so it doesn't take trips that are unhealthy and non-beneficial to your life. If you desire healing or prosperity in your life then focus and tune in on that particular frequency. It is imperative that you make a decision right now to stop talking yourself out of a blessed life and instead say to yourself *"I am worthy."* This is what it means to vibrate on a low frequency giving in to negative emotions that make you doubtful, sad, depressed, undervalued, etc. Which none of these negative emotions are of God as His will for you is to have an abundance of all things in your life? All limiting thoughts must be depleted from the old software in your mind if lasting change is to take place. Demanding and accepting the accountability that a new and more beneficial program be installed that equates a higher level of thinking which will cause your subconscious mind to operate on a healthier system, so go ahead and hit the control alternate delete button. Your mind is like a computer or a file which stores information, ideas, life experiences, habits, memories that society, and other people have tried to conform us to. Some that are beneficial to us and some that have been a huge detriment in shaping our life to what it is today. I think this next and final principle is one of the hardest things for people to do. That is *"receive."* Pride is a factor in this equation. At the end of any given day a person has to come to the conclusion that with God all things are really possible. However, if a person decides to not believe that with God all things are possible their glass will remain full to them but in all actuality it's half full. Leaving you to believe that putting in an excessive amount of effort is the solution to your problem. At this point a person has to forget everything that was once learned in order to grow and expand their thinking to a deeper level of consciousness. Now when that contrary voice tells you otherwise just simply tell that voice to shut up because your higher self knows who's talking. The enemy. There's no need for you to engage in a full blown conversation that can only end up in a debate of doubt and confusion. When you truly receive what God says to be the truth without having the need to see any evidence of it, you are in divine alignment with God convinced that there is no lack or shortage in Him. This is what it means to totally trust our Heavenly Father. His reputation and His winning record speaks volumes to the doubters, naysayers and haters. There is only an abundance of infinite supply waiting for you to learn how to access your personal power then teach others how to do the same. It's graduation time *"Master Teacher."* Jesus was the greatest example to His disciples now the word has been given to us to duplicate by tapping into our higher self as co-creators of God. We are spiritual beings that live in a physical body. Become conscious of this very fact, and wake up from the spiritual coma that the system's, and patterns of this world has caused you to live unconsciously of who you really are as a child of God.

Go ahead now and ask God for what you really want and don't hold back. Have no fear nor insecurities when asking him be confident. He's a loving father not one that imparts fear in His children. With The Spiritual Law Of Asking one must come to the father just like a child in total trust and humility. Asking in faith, in courage and assurance that your father wants to meet all of your needs. How can God give you what you desire if you're afraid to ask Him? You have not because you ask not. It's part of your inheritance as a child of God to prosper in every area of your life but your soul has to prosper first. If this is to hard for you to believe then your life will experience minimal success. Allow your mind to open up to the unlimited possibilities that are in pursuit for your life. The Law Of Increase is not evident in the lives of many people today because they haven't learned how to receive, then detach themselves from the desired outcome they are believing God for. Instead, they continue begging and reminding God of their requests believing this process is called faith in order to get the promise faster. As it will only delay the promise because you are praying from a place of lack and doubt not faith. Faith requires no proof, it just believes no matter how long it takes, because you know at some point it's going to show up. Unfortunately, alot of people have been conditioned to beg in order to get. This isn't a sign of humility nor does it make one appear more spiritual. Instead of doubting, believe, receive the word of God, then let go of all anxiousness trusting that in God's perfect timing it will come to pass. The most important aspect of all is to remove time out of the equation and the desired outcome when you are believing God for anything. Even though you are trusting God for it now not next week, next month, or next year. Now just means it's definitely going to happen you just don't know when. Although, God may allow the birthing of your dream to come to pass during one of these seasons it is for us to believe him "now". There is so much focus on giving in our world today, and less on teaching other's on the importance of being in a position to receive. Shouldn't the person who is blessing other's expect to receive a harvest as they too are planting seed? A farmer plants a seed and expects a harvest. Jesus planted precious seed and we are the harvest of his highest creation *"humanity."* As you go forward in your journey to think like God, becoming a master of divine consciousness, be cognitive of whatever it is that's holding your attention, and thoughts because the thoughts you think will always make an appearance in your life in the form of things, problems, blessings, etc... Regardless if it's good or bad and whether you want it to or not. These are the divine laws of God and as his children who are under His kingdom government, we must learn and effectively operate these laws practically, on a day to day basis, so we can be victorious in this world while we co-exist with others who need our light *"knowledge."* Ready or not your thoughts are going to visit your life at some point or another as it's our responsibility to make sure we're thinking only on the thoughts we want to experience. As the emotions you feel are the accelerator to the manifestation of the promises of God. This is a Universal Law which means your thoughts literally attract your reality by the vibrations and emotions that you are projecting out in the atmosphere from within the space of your heart and your mind. A person has to believe what they are saying. So whatever is taking place in your life you can give yourself all the credit for it because your thoughts, focus, and emotion's has given it permission to live. This is the masterpiece you have designed by way of the thoughts, and images that's been replaying over and over again in your mind. Meditate only on the things that you want to see come to pass in your life. What benefit is it for you to bring yesterday's failure into your today? Why keep talking about how bad it was and how it made you feel? Learn from it and don't live in the hurt of yesterday. Learn to live in the now instead of tomorrow. By neglecting today experiencing a better tomorrow can't show up. If you don't like the way your life is playing out for all the world to see re-write it..........Turn the page and write a new chapter.

"The Importance Of Improving Yourself First"

Isn't it fair to say that a person must always seek to discover different modalities, learn new concepts and ideas on how to improve themselves first? Before extending out to further assist someone else in their personal transformational process? It's not realistic to think that a person can make a positive mark fully in another person's life until you first become that which you wish to see or give to another. A vast majority of people are missing this principle and are finding themselves constantly overcompensating by giving to others while they are bleeding themselves creating habitual defeats, longing for the love, healing and abundance they are giving to others . While perceiving this is what it means to help, instead the infection within you is being passed on to the person you are trying to help. Hindering their healing, development and growth as well as your own. We can't be truly effective in helping anyone until we first help ourselves. Heal your personal wounds by dealing with your brokenness and confront all of your traumas that may have began in your childhood. Self has to be healthy, happy and whole that means the entire aspects of your being spirit, soul, body and your emotion's. Not one can remain locked up and undealt with as it will cause a train wreck in your life. Identify the problem so you can confront it then conquer it.

The Spiritual Law Of Abundance

1. Honor God In Your Giving
2. Learn To Give To Yourself
3. Find Ways To Help Others
4. Practice Getting In The Surrender Mode (Forget It Mode)

You have asked, seeked and knocked now learn how to give it to God while not being concerned about the outcome you're desiring. Have you ever misplaced your keys and tried tirelessly to find them but couldn't? Then as soon as you gave up on trying to find them they showed up in the place you've looked in fifty times. Letting go of trying to control and manipulate how and when the blessing will arrive allows it to come effortlessly and freely into your experience. It's in the same manner that you would naturally open your hand to release balloons in the air. Trusting in God requires the same so release it all to Him, and don't go begging for it again in three days if it hasn't showed up. It's not time yet. Letting go of control issues as you learn to stop begging for things and promises that God has already told you is yours. When a person is oblivious to their birthright they will beg for the things that already belong to them. This is like digging up a seed in the ground after you've planted it, watered it and nurtured it just to see how much it has grown. What sense does that make? Doubt digs up the prayers that one has already prayed. You're choking the life out of what wants to come forth. What if someone gifted you a beautiful car then presented you with the keys and said *"This is yours take it and be blessed."* Would you not take the key and drive off with your car? It's your gift it rightfully belong's to you. Or would you stand there and debate why they shouldn't have bought you the car? Or would you speak words of doubt as to how unworthy you think you are to receive such a gift of this magnitiude? Do you have a problem receiving from others? I use to struggle with this because I equated being spiritual with being a giver only and not a receiver of all things that are good. I felt less worthy when I received from others which is rooted from the spirit of pride. This is why so many people have a problem with allowing others to treat them well. Are you measuring your value and self-worth by being the *"giver"* and not the *"receiver?"* Do you feel less powerful when you receive from others instead of being the person that is doing the giving? The mind has been conditioned to operate from a place of limited potential. This is a perfect time to evaluate then monitor what your belief system is. Prayer has gone forth, faith has been exercised, new information has been learned, positive affirmations have been spoken, visualizations have been written in the space of our mind. With positive emotions sky rocketing through the dimensions in heaven, causing the cosmic world to deliver everything your mind has created to the earth realm, so you can enjoy it with the people you love. We have been placed in this world to *"serve others"* with the gifts and talents that God has given us. Now will you trust God to give you what you've asked him for? It has your name on it and I'm sure you want to claim your prize because no one else can. When you get to heaven how many boxes do you want to see with your name on it that is marked *"Unclaimed Blessings?"* I pray you will never allow others, social circles nor circumstances to influence your decision making and beliefs that will cause you to operate from a low vibrational place. It is you who has had the divine key within you, that unlocks the portal to you having everything you've ever wanted this entire time, due to God's divine nature that lives within you. Your awareness of this fact unlocks the door to that which seems impossible to others, because you now know the truth of the reality you operate in as you are now receiving all the blessings of God. There's nothing that you can do externally to make anything happen faster for yourself because we create from within not from without. When a person learns this principle they will begin to grow after mastering The Law Of Letting Go as faith consummates this relationship for manifestation of answered prayer, because everything that you want and are believing God for already exists within you. All that you are hoping to do and become already exists. It is up to you to discover the truth of who you really are as a divine spirit. When God finished creating everything he desired in the book of Genesis he rested. That day is called The Sabbath. So everything that you want and are praying for already exists, it's time to operate from within our spirit and not the ego. Right now, I want you to take a deep breath in and now breath out. It's like a relationship that you're trying so desperately to hold on to and make work by doing, doing, doing. And the more you try to convince that person you're the best choice for them the more they will create a wall of resistance to keep you out. And treat you like an option instead of a priority. Why does this happen to me people have asked? This happens because you have vibrated negative emotions called neediness, low self-esteem, codependency traits, desperation and insecurity. Let go of the old so a new life can emerge with every wish fullfilment. This is the place where surrender and trust for all things are to be released in the hands of our father God. That means letting go of the obligation of trying so diligently to make something happen regardless of how bad you want it. Due to you coming from a place of not trusting God to do what he said he would do for you only prolongs the answered prayer. Realizing and having an in depth understanding that things will definitely go wrong in our life sometimes but we have to maintain a firm focus on the promises (not the problem) as we express unwavering faith during such difficult seasons in our life. These life lessons challenges us to expand and think on a higher frequency causing us to learn so much about ourselves that we didn't know before. Your perception about things will alter your reality as you begin to look at life from all aspects and from another person's point of view. Not allowing the differences of opinions from others to divide us instead it forces diverse ethnic groups and communities to come together for the purpose of having dialogue as we learn to share and appreciate our individual experiences. If you will make the necessary adjustments to the way you think and feel your life will shift to a place you will be happier to live in. As we have been placed here in this physical world to learn about our creator, then ourselves so we can dominate, govern, rule, and take dominion in our own environment called *"earth"* that our father placed us in. To conclude, if you can learn how to overide fear, and get rid of the *"I'm not good enough complex"* all of those limiting beliefs, and disempowering cycles in your mind will be transformed causing you to attract, and create that life of true abundance that you have always dreamed of, because whatever you are imagining in the present moment will eventually become in the now. Proving that you have mastered the art to think like the creator as this is the only frequency the inner man operates from, in and through. Your God-given human imagination as we all are one with the source who created all things. I am a master of divine consciousness.

"I Am That I Am" has spoken.

Shalom,
Nikki G. MCcray

NOTES

NOTES

NOTES

NOTES

NOTES

NOTES

NOTES

NOTES

NOTES

NOTES